SUCCEEDING AGAINST ALL ODDS

SUCCEEDING AGAINST ALL ODDS

Presented by Sandra Yancey

Presented by: Sandra Yancey

Producer: Ruby Yeh

Editorial Director: AJ Harper

Print Management: Book Lab

Cover Design: Keith Speegle

Book Design & Typesetting: Chinook Design, Inc.

ISBN-13: 978-0-9891792-0-1

Printed in the United States of America

www.eWomenPublishingNetwork.com

Contents

CONTENTS

CONTENTS

CONTENTS

Sandra Yancey

Introduction

In our first collection of inspiring success stories, *Succeeding In Spite of Everything*, I shared a story about the time I contemplated declaring bankruptcy and how my mother's sage advice motivated me to stay the course and find a better approach to building eWomenNetwork.

Shortly after our conversation, I asked one of my girlfriends if she could help me determine my next step. She was running a multi-million dollar business and, though she wanted to help me, she didn't have time. She said, "You can't navigate this alone. You need a business coach."

I'd heard the term before, but the concept was new to me so I hadn't paid much attention to it. When I finally found a business coach, she quoted me a fee of $175 an hour.

I said, "I'm broke now. Could you possibly work with me and then, as I make money, I'll pay you?"

"It doesn't work that way. I'm here; you figure it out," the coach replied. She was right.

Sometimes you need someone to push back and say, "How much do you really want this?" I have this philosophy, the one thing I know to be true about women: When we see something of value, we will figure out how to justify paying for it. If you don't believe me, ask the average woman how many pairs of black pants she has, or black shoes! We all have multiple pairs—different styles, heels, leg cut—even when we don't need another black anything, we still buy the same thing over and over again because we value having options, the right pair of blank pants or black shoes for every occasion.

One day not long after my brief conversation with the business coach, I was folding my kids' clothes in the laundry room, and I ran out of hangers. I went up to my daughter's room and looked through her closet. I said, "Here's something she's outgrown," and

---

When we see something of value, we will figure out how to justify paying for it.

---

put it on the floor so I could use that hanger. I kept going, sliding clothes across the pole and picking out pieces she'd never wear again. "Here's something she wore once, didn't like and now I can't get her to wear it, and here's something with the tags still on that's two sizes too small."

In just a few minutes, I had this little pile of clothes. After pulling more items from my son's room, and my own closet, my little pile was a small mountain.

"Look at all of these fabulous, gently worn or never worn clothes!" I said. I knew someone would want to buy them, so I stuffed everything into three garbage bags and hauled them to the consignment shop, the kind that pays a flat price. This is what I like to call a "God-wink moment."

I asked the clerk, "How much would you give me for all of the clothes?"

She said, "I think I could do $175." *That* was a God-wink—divine intervention, literally. Two hours of my time and a bunch of stuff we no longer needed and I had the exact amount I needed to get started.

I'll never forget my first coaching session. She said, "Tell me how you spend a typical day."

After I walked her through my routine she said, "It's clear that you're caught up in the minutiae of being an entrepreneur. You've got to hire someone to handle the administrative tasks."

I thought, *Don't tell me I spent $175 just to have this woman tell me to find more money to hire somebody!*

"You don't get it," I told her. "I can't hire somebody; I'm broke. You don't know what I had to do to scrape together enough money to hire you."

Without hesitation, my coach said, "You have no choice, Sandra. You need someone to handle all of the things that are bogging you down so that you can focus on the things that make the cash register ring."

When I hired my first employee, I totally freaked out because I knew when I hired her that I didn't have the money to pay her. But sometimes you've got to walk to the edge and jump and then build

---

"What's going on inside of you that's preventing you from putting yourself on the payroll?"

---

your wings on the way down. So I hired an assistant and I'll never forget what it felt like to get to Wednesday back then, scrambling for dollars so that I had enough money in the bank so she could cash her check on Friday.

After three months when I paid both my coach and my assistant, my coach asked me how I was feeling.

"Great!" I said. "I'm making money and I have an employee and I've got you."

I could sense her smile and then she said, "So you know I can't coach you unless you pay me and you know your assistant won't work for you unless you pay her. You value me and you value her—how much do you value yourself? What's going on inside of you that's preventing you from putting yourself on the payroll?"

That was a real wake-up call for me. I started thinking about my money issues—and I really did have a lot of them. It was a process of owning my stuff, working through it, peeling away the layers, sitting with it and crying about it. I had been trying to be of service to others, but for some reason I didn't believe I could make a lot of money doing that. And because I didn't believe it, I wasn't a role model for what I was trying to help others do. No wonder I was struggling!

Working through my money issues was a big turning point for me; once I'd made some progress with that, I started to see my business shift, take root, grow and eventually bloom into a multi-

---

*There is meaning and purpose
behind every obstacle.*

---

million dollar business. Today, eWomenNetwork is the premier women's business network in North America, offering a complete success system for entrepreneurs and their businesses worldwide.

What I came to realize was, my biggest obstacle wasn't lack of skills, or tools, or even a lack of resources. My biggest obstacle was myself. From the moment I launched eWomenNetwork I had been coming up against my own issues and beliefs around self-worth and money *disguised* as lack. And I realize now that, on some level, my obstacles almost always are about "me."

When I encounter a major challenge in life or business, I no longer say, "Who can we hire to solve this?" or "What software will fix this?" Instead I ask myself, "Sandra, what's going on with you that is attracting this obstacle to your life right now?" The more I own my part in all things—the "good" and the "bad"—the easier it is for me to identify the root cause and, in turn, prevent the problem from showing up again in a different way. And it becomes easier for me to stop the "mini-series," as I often refer to it.

Not every problem is about me; sometimes life just deals us a bad hand. We certainly aren't the cause of every wrong turn, or disappointment, or tragic occurrence. We can't control how others choose to show up in the world, but we can control how we react to negative influences, crises and other challenges that come up as we pursue a life of meaning and abundance.

When I titled this book, *Succeeding Against All Odds,* I envisioned a collection of stories that would not only assure people that they could succeed no matter what their circumstances, but would also help them to understand that within our circumstances lies a powerful transformational opportunity.

I knew right away that I wanted to ask my friend Ken Kragen to tell the amazing stories behind his "impossible" goals: "We Are the World"and "Hands Across America." I asked my friends and noted thought-leaders Fabienne Fredrickson and Linda Clemons to share their wisdom. Then, I handpicked thirty-four extraordinary co-authors and, together with my team, asked them to bravely tell the truth about how they realized their dreams despite barriers, perceived limitations and unexpected crises.

As the book began to take shape, I realized most of the stories shared a common thread: All of the remarkable co-authors had, in their own ways, embraced their challenges, and the changes that came along as a result. Just as I did in the early days of my business as I explored my issues around money and value, and as I continue to do with any recurring issue that I come up against, the co-authors dug deep—and found gold.

I'm proud to say that the group of truly fabulous entrepreneurs, business owners and corporate professionals who co-authored this book have all shared inspiring and fascinating stories about how they pushed through challenges to achieve great success *and* then used those challenges to their advantage while in pursuit of their dreams.

There is meaning and purpose behind every obstacle and, if we allow ourselves to go "through" it, we will get to the other side. When we choose instead to "jump over" the obstacle, or take a detour to avoid it, we end up bumping into the same or similar obstacle down the road. Lessons will repeat over and over again, until we not only get it, but also understand how that obstacle wasn't really an obstacle at all, but rather a blessing. You have to go through it, to get to it.

My hope for you, dear reader, is that, as you read the inspiring stories included in this book, you take a look at what has been holding you back and how you've been dealing with it. Are you embracing problems and roadblocks as opportunities to learn more about your own success path, or are you looking for a quick fix? Are you trying to cover up the crises, or are you taking a step back to reflect, trusting that the universe has brought this to you for greater meaning and greater opportunity?

Beneath the surface of every obstacle is the opportunity to see the world a little bit differently, to experience the world a little bit differently and to show up in the world a little bit differently, bringing all of who you are to the planet. Obstacles show up in our lives to make us not only more effective, but also more understanding, more compassionate and, in the end, much more powerful. The financial challenges I encountered in the early years of eWomenNetwork helped me to value mentorship, assistance and my own contributions to the company, which enable me to give my full gifts to the world.

So, if you feel the odds are stacked against you, realize that simply means you have more opportunity than most. Then, with renewed faith and confidence, take action. Let the obstacles work their magic—and then send me your own success story. I already know it will be a good one!

Ken Kragen

The Razor-Edge
of Disaster

Two days before Christmas in 1984, Harry Belafonte called to ask for my help. He'd seen the pictures of children dying in Africa on television and he wanted to organize a concert to raise money for African famine relief.

Inspired to continue the work of Harry Chapin, whom I had managed in the late 70s and early 80s prior to his tragic death, I had done a lot of work in the areas of hunger, poverty and homelessness in America. So I wasn't surprised when Belafonte called to ask for my help. However, I knew there was a better way to raise money and awareness.

Bob Geldof had organized Band Aid, a group of recording artists in the United Kingdom. They'd performed the single "Do They Know It's Christmas?" to raise money for famine relief; the song was playing everywhere.

I said, "Look, Harry, I've tried to put together a benefit concert for the poor for years with no success. Geldof has shown us the way. Let's not reinvent the wheel. We've got bigger artists in the United States than Geldof used in England."

Harry agreed, and from the moment I hung up the phone my primary focus was making this happen. Less than one month later, the biggest recording stars in the world convened at A&M Studios in Hollywood to record "We Are the World."

Thornton Wilder said, "I know that every good and excellent thing in the world stands moment by moment on the razor-edge of danger and must be fought for." Over the years, I've simplified his quote to say, "Every great thing balances at all times on the razor-edge of disaster." Every major project I've taken on has had its crisis moments, throw-in-the-towel-and-quit moments when the odds are stacked so high against you, success truly does seem impossible. I've experienced this in movies I've made, careers I've managed, in almost everything I've done. Yet, when it came down to staying in the game or folding, I've always played my hand.

I stay the course, because I've always had the optimistic belief that there is a way around any problem, and that if what we're doing is, at its core, good and meaningful and important, we will find a way to make it work.

We ran up against several obstacles in creating "We Are the World." Probably one of the wisest decisions I made was to schedule the recording session at midnight on the same night as the American Music Awards (AMA), so a number of the artists who were attending the awards show could come over to A&M Studios directly after the show. The producer of the AMA, Dick

---

Every great thing balances at all times
on the razor-edge of disaster.

Clark, loved the idea. Still, in less than one month we needed to write a hit song, find a producer and convince many of the biggest artists in the country to sign on to sing with each other. We also had to figure out how to deal with all of those egos in one room at the same time! It was daunting, to say the least, because it had never been done in America before.

After hanging up with Belafonte, I drove over to my client Lionel Richie's home and asked him to write the song. I then called Quincy Jones and asked him to produce. He agreed. Then I asked, "Could you get Michael Jackson to perform on it?" Michael was the number-one recording artist in the world at that time, and I knew if we were going to go big, we needed Michael.

In less than an hour, Quincy called back and said, "Michael not only wants to perform, he wants to write the song with Lionel."

With the writers and the producer on board, I took out the record charts, began at the top, and started calling. My goal was to get two artists a day. Four days after his initial call, Harry Belafonte called me back to check on our progress.

I said, "I have half a dozen major artists, a song produced by Quincy and written by Michael and Lionel." Harry was quite blown away!

---

*The night before we were set to record,
we hit a major obstacle that threatened
to thwart the entire project.*

Then, in mid-January, Bruce Springsteen agreed to come to Los Angeles and record with us. I stopped making outgoing calls; I mainly just accepted or turned people down. Springsteen wasn't the biggest-selling artist, but he had the most clout. Once artists heard that Bruce was in, they all wanted to be part of "We Are the World" too.

We still danced on the razor-edge of disaster. For example, there were all the legal issues surrounding these artists, all of whom were signed to major record companies. Getting the lawyers, agents, managers, record companies—and the artists themselves—to agree to use their performances was a massive undertaking.

Then, the night before we were set to record, we hit a major obstacle that threatened to thwart the entire project, or at least greatly diminish it, causing controversy in the process. A manager for one of the rockers approached me at the rehearsal for the AMA. He said, "The rockers don't like the song, and they don't want to stand next to the pop and country artists, so they're not coming."

I said, "Look, we're going to record tomorrow. I'm sorry if you guys don't want to participate."

What happened then was really fascinating. The mutineer rockers decided they had to get the biggest rocker of them all to join them, and that was Springsteen. Again, his involvement proved critical to the success of "We Are the World." When the rockers asked him to leave with them, he said, "I didn't come out to Los Angeles to walk away. I came here to help feed people and save lives, and that's why I'm staying."

The next night, all of the rockers showed up. I'll never forget that night, January 28, 1985, watching all of the limousines pull up to A&M Studios, greeting people as they arrived—forty-five artists in all, each one bigger than the one before. A crowd started to form

We formed USA for Africa, which is still going twenty-eight years later.

at the gates and, at one point, a guy in a leather jacket and cutoff gloves pushed through the crowd. It was Springsteen. He said, "Hey man, I got a great parking space across the street on La Brea."

I still laugh every time I think of him driving his own car over to the studio and looking for parking.

We recorded on Monday and, for the rest of the week, the event was all over the news. I remember waking up on Friday morning and saying to myself, "Wait a second, this is not a charity event where we raise money, hand it over, and then go on with our lives. This is not the end; this is the beginning." It was shocking, realizing the full scope of what had happened, and what we had yet to do.

"We Are the World" ended up being a monster success. Released on March 7, 1985, it became the fastest-selling American pop single in history and the first single to be certified multi-platinum. The song won three Grammys, an American Music Award and a People's Choice Award.

More importantly, because we released an album with unreleased tracks from many of the artists, we raised more than sixty-four-million dollars for African famine relief (compared to the ten-million dollars raised from the single "Do They Know It's Christmas" in England).

More significantly, we formed USA for Africa, which is still going twenty-eight years later. We still fund excellent causes; we still do good work. It wasn't the end at all.

I'm not sure what set me up this way, but my whole life I've always told myself, "think as big as possible." Start big, and you can always back off from it. Even as a high-school kid producing concerts for groups that went on to be number one, I knew that you can't sell anything to anybody unless you get their attention. I've always looked at an idea and thought, "How can we take this up another level?" This philosophy inspired me to spearhead the biggest "impossible" event I've been involved with—so far.

In May of 1985, I was in New York to pick up the first five-million-dollar check from the recording company. I attended a performance of the New York City Ballet, and among the other guests was a publicist who was working on "We Are the World."

I've always looked at an idea and thought,
"How can we take this up another level?"

During intermission, he asked me, "Listen, don't laugh, but what if we strung a single, continuous line of people from New York to Los Angeles, all holding hands and singing the song?"

I'm proud to say my response was, "You know, I'm not laughing. That's just impossible enough to be possible." The idea appealed to my sense of always thinking as big as possible, but I filed it away, because I was getting ready to leave for Africa with the first cargo plane load of supplies—270,000 tons of food, medicine, refrigerators and other necessities.

When I returned to California from that long, exhausting but inspiring trip, a volunteer met me at the airport to drive me home. As we were about to get on the airport's moving walkway, he said, "It's wonderful what you're doing in Africa, but we have a lot of hungry people at home. What are you going to do for America?"

At that moment, the publicist's idea popped back into my head. I talked to various people I was working with on these causes and we started looking for sponsors. By September, Coca-Cola agreed to sponsor "Hands Across America." We were off and running.

If I thought getting forty-five recording artists together to record a song was a huge task, it was nothing compared with figuring out how to get six-and-a-half-million people to stand together all at the same time, from one coast to the other, through seventeen

---

I knew if we filled the line, we would
accomplish all we set out to do.

---

states. Fortunately, it was an off political year, so we were able to hire the organizers who ran campaigns and gathered crowds for speeches—four-hundred paid staff and forty-thousand volunteers in all.

Again, as with all big, important, worthy endeavors, I became well acquainted with the razor-edge of disaster. My board nearly killed the concept, because I rolled ahead and had a new song written for the event without discussing it first. In fact, they almost fired me over that and the fact that we had no insurance. I had filled the board with big stars and their reps, so there were a lot of egos in the room. Most people were worried about their own financial situations. If we were sued, they were big targets. Less than two months from the big event, after we'd run Super Bowl ads promoting "Hands Across America," with two-million people already signed up, the board gave me one week to find insurance to cover the board and the event. Otherwise, they would cancel it. The problem was only one insurance company in the entire country would even consider issuing a policy to cover the event, and it was unlikely it would agree to it.

As I took the red-eye flight to New York to a meeting with this company, I suddenly remembered that the man I was to meet who would decide our fate was a big Kenny Rogers fan. So, early that morning I called Kenny. I said, "As soon as the insurance office opens, would you call this guy and tell him how important it is to give us this insurance." A couple of hours later Kenny called me and said, "He loved that I called him and said he will do the insurance."

The whole thing could have folded at any time. But, the biggest issue of all was filling the line. My motto throughout the process was: "Fill the line and forget everything else." I knew if we filled the line, we would accomplish all we set out to do—raise major dollars, call attention to the plight of the homeless and hungry in America and make strides toward trying to solve these issues.

On Sunday, May 26, 1986, the line began in Manhattan. It began in Battery Park with a young homeless girl, who held the hand of her homeless mother, who in turn held mine. There we stood, looking out at the Statue of Liberty, as the line began to form. It was four rows deep along the West Side Highway, and across the George Washington Bridge. It stretched across state after state, even going through the White House portico with

---

*To do the impossible, you must do something
that is unique or special, something of
substance and something unexpected.*

President and Mrs. Reagan in the line. It stretched across lakes, with people in scuba gear holding hands, and across miles of desert. It went all the way to the *Queen Mary* in Long Beach, California.

People came over the hill at the last minute to fill those lines. At a break in the line, a bus driver stopped his bus and made everyone get off and hold hands to fill the gap. A man who was driving cattle put his steers in another break in the line and had people hang onto the horns. We had five marriages in the line and one birth. From coast to coast, six-and-a-half-million Americans holding hands at the same time—it was really quite incredible.

We raised thirty-four-million dollars from the actual event, increased awareness and changed the whole view of how we handle the issues of hunger and homelessness in this country. We even got President Reagan to release eight-hundred-million dollars he was holding back that was earmarked to feed women and infants.

When I teach at UCLA, or speak at the eWomenNetwork Conference, or anywhere, I talk about the fact that "to do the impossible, you must do something that is unique or special, something of substance and something unexpected." On the word "unexpected," a full marching band comes blasting through the room.

I say, "Now, I have your attention. Where's the marching band in everything you're doing? Or your version of it?" It can be any number of things that get people's attention, but it must be audacious. Big!

What is your WOW factor? It's there. You have it. You just need to find it.

Whenever you think, "Nobody will do that, or buy that or accept that," remember that it may simply be impossible enough to be possible. Remember that all the best things court the razor-edge of disaster. And, remember dozens of artists uniting in song to feed the hungry, and millions of Americans holding hands to do the same.

If it's a good thing, there's a way to do it—and the bigger and more impossible, the better.

A graduate of Harvard Business School, Ken Kragen's illustrious career far transcends the music and entertainment industries, where he has spent many incredibly successful years. He has managed some of the world's most important entertainers, including Kenny Rogers, Lionel Richie, Trisha Yearwood, Olivia Newton John, The Bee Gees and many others. He was the creator and organizer of "We Are the World," "Hands Across America" and Cisco System's "NetAid." More than ninety-five percent of the acts he managed became stars, and ninety percent of the projects he created and spearheaded have achieved success.

Ken has consulted for leading corporations and many non-profit organizations, as well as the Clinton campaign. He produced a significant portion of President Clinton's 1992 Inauguration. He has lectured at Harvard Business School, USC, Loyola, the University of Tennessee and many other schools. For years, he taught courses in UCLA's Extension Program and most recently to undergraduates at UCLA's Herb Alpert School of Music. His courses are based on his unique concepts of career development and formulas for advancing projects to a higher level of excellence.

Among dozens of awards, Ken has been celebrated by the NAACP, the Los Angeles Advertising Women and the Boys & Girls Clubs of America. He received two MTV Awards, an American Music Award and several Emmy nominations. He is most proud of receiving the United Nations Peace Medal for the creation of "Hands Across America" and "We Are the World."

Ken has served on several charity Boards, including The Mr. Holland's Opus Foundation, Communities In Schools and USA for Africa. He is the author of the bestselling book Life is a Contact Sport. *To connect with Ken, visit www.KenKragen.com.*

Fabienne Fredrickson

Dust Yourself Off
and Try Again

Late in 1999, I returned to my tiny 250-square-foot apartment to find a piece of paper taped to my door: Eviction Notice.

In New York City, when you default on your rent for a few months, the eviction notice isn't slipped quietly under your door or tucked into an envelope. I knew it was coming, but to see it right there in black and white for my two sets of neighbors to see was one of the lowest points in my life. The humiliation was unbearable as my stomach twisted into a sick feeling that had become all too familiar.

A few months before, I had quit my advertising sales job and started a private nutrition practice out of my apartment. I had put up my shingle and landed a few clients right away, but not as many as I needed to pay my fourteen-hundred-dollar-a-month midtown-Manhattan rent.

My few clients were getting great results, and I knew I was good at what I did, but the money wasn't coming in fast enough. I was floating my life, my business and basically my whole existence on several credit cards while doing my best to get more out there to market myself. But with few new clients coming in, it got to a point where I was barely making my minimum credit card payments.

After a while, my cards became maxed out, and that's when the credit card companies started calling, practically on a daily basis, to find out when they could expect a payment. I stopped answering the phone and each time I heard the voicemails, my stomach would turn into knots.

This is when I began waking up with what I now call my three-a.m.-I-don't-have-enough-clients sweats. I kept saying, "What have I done? Why did I leave my high-paying corporate job just to struggle to find clients? How will I stay in my apartment if I don't get more clients FAST?"

I tossed and turned every night, barely getting enough sleep, until I couldn't take it any longer. One night at three a.m., I called my father in France and told him that, yes, indeed, I had clients, and they were getting great results, but that I didn't have enough clients and that things were looking really bleak. I cried, feeling ashamed and embarrassed that my gamble and my leap of faith hadn't worked out.

After I explained my situation, he said, "Fabienne, if there's one thing I know about you, it's that when you want something, and you want it badly enough, nothing is going to stop you from getting it. So, just figure out how you're going to get clients, and then go and do it." Now, to some, that might seem like an obvious comment, a "duh" moment. But for me, it was a defining moment.

My stomach twisted into a sick feeling
that had become all too familiar.

I knew that I wasn't cut out to work for anyone else, that my freedom was the most important thing to me and having tasted how sweet self-employment was (the good parts of it) I realized I was no longer able to work for anyone else again. I was officially unemployable and unwilling to go back into the corporate world. This was literally a life-and-death situation for me. I had to make this work.

The next afternoon, I walked through Union Square on my way to the health food store to buy some things for an upcoming cooking class. I was at my lowest of the lows, but trying to keep my spirits up, so I was listening to the radio on my headphones. A chorus in a song by Aaliyah came on.

If at first you don't succeed
Dust yourself off and try again
You can dust it off and try again... ©

I let the words sink into my soul, hoping to glean a little bit of confidence to keep going. The next song that came on the radio was just okay, so I turned the dial. Again, Aaliyah's song "Try Again" came on. I was surprised, but I listened to it, allowing it to boost my faith that perhaps it was a message I needed to hear:

If at first you don't succeed
Dust yourself off and try again
You can dust it off and try again... ©

Once the song was over, again, I turned the radio dial to find another song I liked. And that's when I stopped right in my tracks. My eyes welled up in tears that then streamed down my face. I couldn't believe it. The song played again for a third time in a row.

If at first you don't succeed
Dust yourself off and try again
You can dust it off and try again... ©

I put my hands on my face, sobbed like a baby in the middle of Union Square Park and was clear that this was a divine sign, one that was unmistakable, that I had to keep going, against all odds. I knew I wasn't alone on this journey anymore; I now had the faith to not give up and I realized that there was a reason I was meant to be in business.

That's when I made a commitment to fill my practice, no matter what it was going to take. I was unwilling to throw in the towel, no matter what I saw in front of me.

I decided to take a no-excuses approach and immerse myself in absolutely everything that had to do with getting clients. I read every book on marketing and networking I could get my hands on. I took every course that was available that would teach me how

©Aaliyah. "Try Again." *Romeo Must Die: The Album.* Virgin Records US, 2000.

to bring in additional clients. Essentially, I decided to become an expert on how to get clients.

I said to myself, *I need a verifiable, repeatable process to find good clients who pay me well, and I need it now.* What I realized in the process was: Plenty of people were teaching different aspects of client attraction, but there were two problems.

First, not every "marketing guru" had best practices for what it's like to be a solo-entrepreneur. In fact, many of them were teaching things they'd learned in books and not through their own

---

**I decided to become an expert
on how to get clients.**

---

practice and experience. So, not everything worked! And most of it was inauthentic, made up of slick techniques that seemed out of integrity to me.

Frankly, it was exhausting to apply something and not know whether it would actually produce results. Sometimes, I would put my head on the pillow at night with my tears rolling down my face and soaking into the pillow.

The other thing I realized was that not everything I needed to attract clients was available in one place. I had to go to one person for guidance on networking, to another for learning how to craft my ideal client profile, yet another for advice on creating a signature talk that would attract new clients and how to craft that talk, someone else regarding closing the sale, another expert on creating a web site and brochure, and the list goes on and on.

It was hugely frustrating to be shelling out more money to get an incomplete picture of what it takes to fill one's practice. But I persevered. And every time something actually worked and I got a client from it, I would put it in this imaginary "THIS WORKS" box. Each time something did not work, I would discard it.

I was looking for a system that was easy to implement and that worked every time, so that each time I wanted new clients, I could just put a few things in place and be guaranteed new clients. That's when the earliest version of The Client Attraction System® was born.

Lo and behold, within less than eight months, I had filled my private nutrition practice to full capacity: thirty clients. I was on top of the world! My perseverance and my no-excuses approach had worked! I had created a system that was guaranteed to give me clients consistently. I was able to pay down my credit card bills and feel happy being self-employed. When you have clients, life becomes really good.

My nutrition colleagues heard about my rapid success and started taking me to the side, whispering, "Fabienne, how do you have thirty clients in less than a year and I've only had three this year? What am I doing wrong? Can you help me?"

I'd give them two or three things to do and ask them to call to tell me how it went.

Every time, the nutritionist called me a few weeks later saying "Woo-hoo! I got a new client! Can you give me another tip?"

Soon, they started asking to become clients in my six-month nutrition program, but they said they didn't want to learn about nutrition. Instead, they wanted my marketing advice. And each time, they would get new clients and make more money.

No matter what you see in front of you, anything can be shifted.

Word spread to chiropractors, acupuncturists, personal trainers and then financial advisors, photographers and wedding planners that I'd created The Client Attraction System® and they too hired me.

That's when I had an epiphany. The thing I enjoyed most about being in business for myself wasn't teaching clients how to cook brown rice so it doesn't stick to the pot or how to make tofu taste yummy. It was actually the marketing.

I began to love marketing and how it can change lives when it is done with authenticity, integrity and love. I also realized that there were countless people like me, millions, in fact, who had opened up their businesses because they wanted freedom and to be catalysts in people's lives, but who had never been shown a proven client attraction system to follow.

A year later, I closed my nutrition practice, opened ClientAttraction.com and made a commitment to dedicate the rest of my professional life to teaching other self-employed sole practitioners how to get more clients in record time. Today, just a little over ten years later, it has evolved into The Client Attraction Business School™, the largest of its kind in the world, and has become a multi-million-dollar business serving solo-entrepreneurs around the globe.

The company has since repeatedly been featured on *Inc. Magazine's* list of America's Fastest-Growing Private Companies (Top 100 of all female-owned American companies in 2011), and I was honored to receive the Stevie® Award (it's like the Oscar of business) for Female Entrepreneur of the Year in 2012. Best of all, my husband was able to quit his unsatisfying job on Wall Street to run this business with me. We model for our three little kids that they too can create anything they want in their lives, if they believe in themselves and do whatever it takes.

Here's what I've learned about life and business: My father was right. When you want something and you want it badly enough, nothing can stop you from getting it. When you take a no-excuses approach to changing your own situation, and you take personal responsibility for your results, you can achieve anything, even if it's against all odds. That's when miracles happen.

If you had given me a glimpse of my future as I was lying in bed, tossing and turning at three a.m. over ten years ago, I would have ignored the inner gremlin and believed in my abilities and myself more. I would never have thought about giving up.

Know this: No matter what you see in front of you, anything can be shifted, especially when you have faith and you believe in the unseen. In fact, this is the mantra on my wall both at home and at the office:

I positively expect great results
no matter what I see in front of me.
The universe is rearranging itself
for my best interest right now.

I hope you too will begin to look at your life in this way. If you do, you will achieve anything you like, even against all odds.

Fabienne Fredrickson is an inspirational mentor to thousands of business owners worldwide. She is an author, international speaker and founder of The Client Attraction Business School™ and ClientAttraction. com, ranked repeatedly by Inc. Magazine *as one of America's Fastest-Growing Private Companies. As one of the most influential marketing and success mindset thought-leaders and business coaches in the world, Fabienne's unique ability is getting entrepreneurs to take immediate marketing action on a systematic basis to produce dramatic results in less time than they would on their own. She's dedicated her life to helping entrepreneurs and business owners create a legacy of service through their businesses, adding value to the world in a lasting way and creating breakthrough paradigm shifts in their mindsets and their personal incomes.*

To connect with Fabienne and sample her work at no charge, you may order her FREE audio CD, "How to Attract All the Clients You Need" and receive her free weekly training videos on attracting more high-paying clients and increasing your income at www.ClientAttraction. com.

Linda Clemons

Listen With Love

How many entrepreneurs or business professionals come up short of their dreams because they think they "can't sell" or are afraid of sales? Too many—maybe you'd count yourself among them. Fear of sales is rarely about just one thing, but those who "don't like" sales are usually people who have anxiety about putting themselves out there. They don't want to ask, or make the pitch.

This chapter isn't about how to fix all of that. Though I have taught thousands of people how to become multi-million dollar producers by changing how they communicate with words, and with their bodies, the first essential sales strategy everyone must learn has nothing to do with talking. Success in sales is first and foremost about listening.

If cultivated, the art of listening—to prospects, clients, partners, everyone—will ensure that your great idea, your vision, your mission in life and in business, is a resounding success, no matter what your circumstances.

In June of 1994, a simple outpatient surgical procedure put me in a coma. Due to an overdose of anesthesia, my heart stopped and I had to be brought back to life. My family and friends, my fellow church members, all were prepared for my death. But after a week, I opened my eyes and began talking.

I believe something bigger and greater than me decreed that my mission and my purpose in life was not yet complete. I was already a student of body language. The week in a coma when everything stopped kicked my spirit of discernment and observation up a notch. Noticing and appreciating the little things in life allowed me to focus on individuals; to discern the most powerful things about them; to listen until it hurts; to listen so that I can hear what is not being said.

In my work as a sales trainer, I find that salespeople are busy broadcasting what they have to offer; they don't tune in to find out what's going on really going on beneath the layers of the customer. Entrepreneurs are often so excited and elated to be able to sell their products and their services that they do seventy to eighty percent of the talking; they should be doing seventy to eighty percent of the listening.

Let's say we're at a networking event. Everybody is coming up to you with business cards and you're handing out your cards as fast as you can. I come up and say "You must be a rock star—you've got so many people around you. What do you do for a living?"

You tell me everything you do. I listen very intently so I can learn what's important to you.

*A simple outpatient surgical
procedure put me in a coma.*

Because I've listened so patiently, you say, "Oh my gosh, Linda, I've been doing most of the talking. What do you do?"

I answer, "Strangely enough, what you do complements what I do. You shared with me that you help individuals make their passion and their purpose into a viable business model. I'm a sales and body language expert, so I can help the people you're working with get their message, their product or service, out to the rest of the world." I've not pitched you. Instead, I've presented what you do in such a way that you are apt to say, "You know what, we should work together."

Success comes when we can hear the inaudible and see the invisible. We do this by taking the time to listen with love, listen with intent and focus. We need to get a connection from heart to heart, mind to mind, breath to breath, so the customer can say, "Oh my gosh, we've been to three different presentations and all three products are similar, but no one gets us the way you do." Unless we can do that, we're just spinning our wheels.

I've heard people say, "I don't care if you give it to me for free, I don't want it."

And the salesperson doesn't get it; they try to bring in a manager or offer bonuses or lower the price. In reality, the salesperson didn't build a value; they didn't check the temperature throughout the presentation to be sure they were making the connection and building value.

Salespeople are busy broadcasting what they have to offer.

Let's look at a couple, Mary and Steve, at a resort sales presentation. Mary leans forward, listening intently. Then she leans over to Steve and says, "We can use this, Honey."

Steve is sitting back in the chair, arms folded and says, "If you want it, I guess that's it. Where's the men's restroom?"

Some salespeople might think they've clinched the sale because "if Mama ain't happy, nobody's happy."

But I would say to Mary, "Let me ask you this. Are you buying this to be able to save money and go on vacation? Or do you think this would be something you and Steve can use to strengthen your marriage?"

I saw what might have been invisible to another salesperson. I saw how Steve kept himself aloof while Mary was trying to lean closer. I heard what might have been inaudible to someone else: that Mary said "we" and "us," but Steve didn't.

I realized that there could be some possible issues in the marriage and that Mary was trying to buy this resort property so that as husband and wife they could take a vacation together and remain together.

Unless we can resolve the issue and get both parties on board, a later conversation will take place in the car.

Steve will say something like, "You bought this vacation property, so I guess we're not going to get the living room set you wanted." And then the sale gets cancelled.

You haven't earned the right to ask for that order until you understand the customer's state of mind, or what's in the customer's

---

Success comes when we can hear the inaudible and see the invisible.

---

heart. You haven't fully connected with the people in your business or personal life until you've learned to see the invisible and hear the inaudible.

Perhaps the worst example of not listening occurred when I was training a salesperson—we'll call her Julie.

During her presentation, Julie asked her potential customer, "Sally, besides the money, what prevents you from buying this timeshare today for you and your family?"

Sally answered, "I have cancer and have only have only a few months to live."

Julie just kept on talking. She said, "Okay, let me show you these other packages."

Instead of listening and thinking: *Why is Sally here on this presentation, if she only has months to live? Let me ask some careful questions that will reveal more. Maybe she's here because she wants to spend her remaining months enjoying vacation time and doing things with her grandchildren.*

Julie lost that opportunity and the sale with it.

It's important to listen intentionally with co-workers, with friends, with loved ones, with spouses, with children. Learn how to connect with someone and create an invisible umbilical cord between you and another human being. That's the deep connection.

That's the first connection we have coming into this world. When you create that connection, human to human, you're almost one. And when you have that connection, putting yourself out there to share what you have to offer is the easiest, most natural thing in the world.

During a break at a presentation for a large not-for-profit organization, one of the board members told me privately, "I'm having a challenge with my son. I can't connect with him."

Now, when you ask a person to give you an example, they will relive the experience, so I asked her to tell me about a specific situation. When she did that, you should have heard her tone!

I told her, "When you say it in that tone, you are demeaning the young man in your life."

I gave her some strategies on how to deal with her tone of voice, how to listen. I told her not to stand over him, but to sit down with him. I asked that she not interrupt.

I told her, "I want you to eat every word," meaning lean forward with your mouth slightly open. Later she shared that listening from the heart saved her relationship with her son.

When you listen with love, with an open heart, all things are possible. A new client, a big order, an important business connection, a renewed relationship; it all begins with listening. And you can do that, right? You may not feel ready to make a

---

*Learn how to connect with someone
and create an invisible umbilical cord
between you and another human being.*

---

big presentation, or ask for the sale, but you can learn how to pay attention, to see the invisible and hear the inaudible.

Imagine how your business would improve if you truly understood your prospects, partners and clients. Now think about how could your business grow if they, in turn, felt that you "got them," that you knew them on a heart level, or maybe even on a soul level. Once you've cultivated this powerful and effective skill, you'll soon hear information that might surprise you—new insights about your industry, or your products or services, insights that could help you succeed not only against all odds, but beyond your wildest dreams.

Linda Clemons is one of the most respected sales and body language experts in the world today. She is the CEO of Sisterpreneur, Inc.® an international business organization to empower and enrich women entrepreneurs. Her extensive mastery of non-verbal communication has assisted many individuals in achieving personal and professional success. Her global clientele and audiences include federal and state governmental agencies such as the White House, United States Customs Department and the FBI; Major League Baseball, Southwest Airlines, MGM and Nestle; and countless hotels and resorts around the world as well as Fortune 500 companies.

Linda has received many recognitions and honors including: the Sagamore of the Wabash, the highest civilian honor in the state of Indiana; Office Depot Entrepreneur of the Year award; WOW, the Women of Wealth Mentoring Award; and a listing in the United States Congressional Record.

Often known as the "Queen of Networking," her work with entrepreneurs and sales forces throughout the country has allowed Linda to make achievers of those who are willing to learn. Because of her mastery of motivation and her vast sales and business expertise, Linda is a very popular trainer/speaker. She travels the world as a master sales strategist and body language expert. She also speaks on motivation and empowerment.

Linda is an accomplished playwright and author who is certified in analytical interviewing, a process used to detect deception and gather data from witnesses, hostages and victims. In addition to being active in her church and community, Linda is a speaker with the Zig Ziglar corporation. Connect with Linda at www.LindaClemons.com.

Lisa Copeland

Color Outside the Lines

"If FIAT of Austin can sell a hundred new cars in a single month, Lisa, you can meet anybody you want. I'll bring them out—it's on me," Tim Kuniskis, head of FIAT brand NAFTA told me.

It was early 2012 and, though it had only been one-and-a-half years since we opened the Austin dealership, it looked as though we had a good chance of breaking the North American sales record. FIAT owns Chrysler, Ferrari, Maserati and other brands, so I knew I could meet any celebrity—George Clooney, Jennifer Lopez, Clint Eastwood; Tim had all kinds of people in his stable.

But I didn't want to meet a celebrity. I wanted to meet someone I truly admired, someone who had influenced and, in my opinion, rescued the United States' automotive industry. On my bucket list I had three revolutionary people I was determined to meet in my lifetime, three men whom I consider to be my absolute heroes: former President Ronald Reagan; former President and CEO of Chrysler, Lee Iacocca; and Sergio Marchionne, the Chairman and CEO of FIAT S.P.A, Inc. and Chrysler Corporation.

I was fortunate enough to see Ronald Reagan at the 1984 Republican Convention in Dallas, Texas. My father was a delegate. Meeting Sergio Marchionne was actually a real possibility—only one small hurdle to cross: We must break the NAFTA FIAT sales record.

So I said, "The only person I want to meet is our Chairman and CEO, Sergio Marchionne. That's it. Just him, no one else will do."

Unbeknownst to Mr. Marchionne, Kuniskis and I made a bet, and we went into sales overdrive at FIAT of Austin. We broke the North American sales record in April of 2012, and Sergio Marchionne made good on Tim's commitment. He personally came to Austin to give us the award.

Meeting him was the absolute highlight of my automotive career. He is the real deal, so powerful, yet so kind. From this meeting, I could tell that he pays attention to every detail of his business, even the smallest segment, that is, the FIAT brand, NAFTA.

Mr. Marchionne arrived with a security detail, and the international press corps covered the event. He held a private meeting with us, and the highlight for me was the moment he told the audience and the press, "Lisa is also an incredible salesperson

---

I was a fashion major selling cars in pencil skirts and four-inch heels.

---

herself, an excellent manager and a dynamic leader, and what she and her team have achieved here at the FIAT of Austin dealership is unprecedented." He was so genuine, so complimentary; I was holding back tears. After our meeting, he said to me, "I'm so proud of you." *Sergio Marchionne is proud of me? Truly a defining moment!*

If, when I started out in auto sales twenty-four years ago, you would have told me that I would one day receive an award from one of the most influential men in this industry, I would have said, "No way." And, if you would have told me that: We would earn our award with a sales team which, before working for us, had never sold a car; a sales team that sold from a six-thousand-square-foot dealership in a retail shopping center; using management and sales techniques that we developed in order to attract young people— bright young women—into a career in auto sales, techniques that would be heralded and studied by our industry, I would have laughed out loud.

The Dallas Chevy dealership I walked into in 1987 was a different world. I was twenty years old, a fashion major with plans to make it big as a designer, and I needed a car to get to school. (Public transport was not an option at the time.) I had wrecked my car, and because I cared more about buying clothes than paying my car insurance, my dad told me I needed to "figure out" how I would get my next car.

Someone told me that people in auto sales were given a demo car to drive, so I went to the dealership where my friend worked and applied. They were not interested. But I kept at it. How else would I get a car? After three interviews and groveling for a thirty-day trial period, I was off to the races.

I was a fashion major selling cars in pencil skirts and four-inch heels. Every day, I lived in fear that I would lose my car and my job. I was reminded daily that I was lucky to be a sales professional for this organization, because "this is not a women's business." I was told, "Look pretty and the sales will come."

The guys hated me; they didn't want me there. Not only did they not offer me support, they actively tried to get me to leave. One day

---

I was not in the sales business; I was in the people business.

I walked in to find they'd put a baby alligator in my desk! The circumstances were not ideal, but the challenging environment motivated me to dig in and figure out how to make a go of it in this male-dominated business.

My very first sale backed out at the last minute, because I had mistakenly told them the car included a full-size spare tire. My sales manager said, "If you ever lie to a customer again, you're fired."

I knew I hadn't lied to anybody—I just didn't know enough about cars. I went to the bathroom and cried my eyes out.

When I came back onto the floor he said, "I can tell you've been crying. If you ever cry again, I'm going to fire you."

"All right," I replied, squaring my shoulders. From that moment on I said everything my sales manager told me to say. I had to survive, and I didn't know any better, so I talked to everyone, especially the customers no one else would talk to—the woman with six kids who walked in by herself, the Hispanic man who didn't speak English, the couple who drove up in an old beater.

Very quickly I learned to never stereotype a customer. They've been stereotyped their whole lives; what they need is service, attention and respect. I started making sales, because I really

---

*If you never ask, you will never
receive what you deserve.*

---

liked my customers and I wanted to take care of them. I built relationships with them.

Within a year, I never had to stand up front on the floor with fifty men to find a new customer; my business was one-hundred-percent referral based. When you treat everybody equally, they will send you referral business for years to come. Because of this, the gay and lesbian community was my number-one referral source—they didn't even bother with the guys up front.

It was then that I understood that I was not in the sales business; I was in the people business—and I wanted to be with the people, not stuck in a back room designing dresses. I figured out that I loved it and dug my heels in deep.

After a year, the men who resented me for being hired now resented me for my success. They wanted to know my secret. Eventually, I was promoted from the sales floor to the finance office, then to finance manager and then sales manager. But, over the course of my career, there were promotions within dealerships that I knew I should have been mine, because I had a stronger skill set and more expertise, which were given to my less-qualified male counterpart.

Every time I was passed over, I would approach the senior-level manager and say, "I am the best person for this job; why am I being passed over? If you give me the job, I'm going to get it done. It isn't fair to judge me on the fact that I have young children at home. I've never not shown up for work. I'm going to do everything the man is going to do times ten. I want the job." Every step up the ladder, I've had to have this conversation.

The most high-powered and best-paying careers are typically male dominated, because women are people pleasers. We do it with our friends; we do it with our families; and, tragically for our careers, we do it at work. We don't want to ruffle feathers or hurt feelings. We want harmony, not conflict. Worst of all, we are afraid to ask for what we want—the promotion, a better work environment, a chance at trying something new. In my opinion, this behavior is precisely what keeps women from excelling in male-dominated fields.

Nationally, women hold 2 percent of the jobs in auto sales. Only 3.8 percent of Fortune 500 companies have female CEOs. If we're going to have more women in the "C" suites (CEO, CFO, and so on), women are going to have to be willing to have their own version of that conversation. We are going to have to give up our people-pleasing ways and ask for what we want—for what we deserve.

Coming up the ranks as a sales manager, I tried to mentor the new sales people, both male and female. I noticed the women did not last, primarily for the same reason I almost didn't—no female leadership or mentorship.

I told myself, "If I ever have a position of true leadership or power, I will change things."

When I became the general manager of the number-one FIAT dealership in North America, I set out to do just that. I was lucky that my mentor/boss/partner, Nyle Maxwell, trusted me to do it my way. We hired young, inexperienced and teachable people, and offered them what was never offered to me: mentorship and training.

Every day I tell them, "Work hard and someday you may have my job." My dream is to raise up young leaders and give them obtainable goals and hope for a bright future. This is a great industry and if you excel truly the sky is the limit. I am living proof.

At FIAT of Austin, we make it easier for women with children to have careers by offering flex time and job shares. We encourage those who want to to finish college and get their degrees, to do whatever it takes to make them whole persons. We have taught our staff a true love of our brand, of each other and of the auto industry. I am proud to say that when we move into our new facility more than half of our sales team and management team will be female. This is why, in 2013, *Automotive News Magazine* named FIAT of Austin one of the best dealerships to work for in North America. We colored outside the lines and became the toast of the auto industry!

I still think about that June day in 2012, when I met my hero, Sergio Marchionne. Every moment of the experience is imprinted in my mind—and I also have a visual reminder that's hard to miss.

Before he left the event, Mr. Marchionne asked, "What can I do for you, Lisa?"

"My dream is to own a hot-pink car," I replied. "That car will forever remind me of this day and this amazing accomplishment that this young sales team achieved against all odds."

Mr. Marchionne turned to Tim Kuniskis and said, "Build it."

The Copeland Edition FIAT 500, my custom-built pink car, sits on my showroom floor. Every time I look at it, I'm reminded that someone of Sergio Machionne's caliber made that for me, because we achieved something amazing. Because I asked. I believe and teach my team that, if you never ask, you will never receive what you deserve, that any meeting could change your destiny or your career path or your life.

I am very involved with the Girl Scouts of Central Texas, and let me tell you, those girls know how to be persistent. Standing outside of the mall in front of their little folding table, they learn really quickly that if they gracefully take a "no" (as girls are taught to do), people will ignore them. Selling Girl Scout cookies teaches them how to handle rejection at a young age and how to gracefully rebound from it. I believe it's the best sales training in the world!

I once had a little girl come to me crying. She said, "Six people said 'no.' Nobody will buy from us. Can we please go home?"

I said, "No, you can't go home. Ask six more."

Dare to put yourself out there. Don't be afraid to say, "I'm worthy of success." Don't be afraid to color outside the lines, to ask for that job even though you'll be the only girl on the sales floor, to ask for the promotion, to think outside the box in order to make your industry a better place for all people. Ask for your own dream client, or job or even something as crazy as your own pink car. And, if you ask and you get a "no," don't let them see you sweat. Just get back up and ask again. We are responsible to ourselves and everyone who is watching us to create our own success and write our own destiny.

Make the ask.

Lisa Copeland is one of the most respected faces in automotive sales. With over twenty years of success within a male-dominated industry, Lisa is a dedicated pioneer for women on the automotive sales floor. As a member of the National Chrysler Dealer Council and the managing partner of FIAT of Austin, she represents the North American pulse of the FIAT brand. Under Lisa's management, FIAT of Austin became the first FIAT studio in North America to sell one hundred Fiat 500s in a single month. In 2013, Chrysler Group CEO Sergio Marchionne honored Lisa for record-breaking FIAT 500 sales.

Lisa's extensive knowledge of hiring, training and retaining diverse candidates has positioned her as an expert in sales and management. She has been featured in prominent publications, including the Wall Street Journal, The New York Times, Marie Claire *and* Automotive News. *In 2012,* Austin Business Journal *named her one of the Five Most Powerful Women in Austin. She is currently writing a book about the unique approach she used to achieve unprecedented success in sales and business.*

Lisa is also the co-founder of Women Impacting the Nation and The Project 19 Foundation, two non-profit organizations dedicated to forwarding leadership roles for women. As the creator of BuyingCarsHerWay.com, she offers inside information to the female consumer in an effort to empower women as consumers. Serving the community runs in the Copeland family. Lisa's daughter, Allix, is a special education teacher; her son, JT, followed her career path and entered the auto industry. Connect with Lisa at www.Lisa Copeland. com.

Sheila Wysocki

Improve Your Odds

Overarching evil seemed to suck the air from the courtroom. I stared at the beast of a man who had raped and stabbed to death my college roommate, Angela Samota. As I sat listening to the same gruesome details of what happened to Angie, it was hard to take my eyes off of the man who changed the course of my life. Angela had long brownish hair and eyes that sparkled. She was vivacious and popular and smart, too—she was studying computer science and electrical engineering at Southern Methodist University in Dallas, Texas—and back then, in 1984, few women entered those fields.

Angela had come home after a night out with friends about 1:30 a.m. Shortly after arriving home, she had called her boyfriend to say that a stranger was in her apartment—he'd asked to use the phone and the bathroom. She had promised to call back right away. When she didn't her boyfriend had first tried calling her, then gone to the condo, and finally called the police. They had entered her condo at 2:17 a.m., only to find her body.

The police had suspects. All but one were ruled out because their blood types didn't match the evidence. The police asked me to help find evidence against the last suspect. I talked to him on the phone and even had dinner with him in a restaurant, but he didn't say anything incriminating. He took a lie detector test and passed it, but after a "second look" the police changed their minds and said he had failed it. Without more evidence, the case went dead, but many of us believed he was the perpetrator.

I moved to Nashville, Tennessee, had a family and went on with my life. But I never forgot Angie and never forgot that her killer was still free.

For twenty-six years, I waited for justice, making hundreds of phone calls to the Dallas police department, pushing for evidence to be tested. Hoping that would give me access to the DNA samples stored in Dallas, I got a private investigator's license. Having struggled with dyslexia, this was not the easiest of tasks. To help me pass the test to obtain my license, my oldest child, Charlie, who was fourteen at the time, read the handbook to me.

In 2004, while doing a Bible study, I saw a vision of Angie sitting at the end of my bed. She didn't say anything, but the vision of her was so clear I felt her presence physically. I knew it was time to solve the case to ultimately let Angie rest in peace. I kept up my calls, and asked friends to call, requesting action.

Finally, the DNA samples were tested. The DNA belonged, not to that earlier suspect, but to a man who was already in prison, on a charge of rape.

He had been out on parole from another
rape charge when he murdered Angie.

He had been out on parole from another rape charge when he murdered Angie. Now he sat before me looking at the horrendous crime scene photographs as though they were pictures from a family album.

Throughout the trial, I thought: *Without warning, her life changed in an instant. Without warning, she opened the door and let this beast in. Without warning, he stabbed her. She needed to fight back; she needed to fight back.*

I knew that one out of every four women will be raped; one out of every six men will be raped. And that's a national statistic based on reported rapes. How many go unreported? I thought about violent robberies, spousal assaults, murders. Solving the case and punishing the criminal is fine, but can't we do more to prevent these tragedies? Can't we increase the odds of avoiding or surviving an attack? That's when the idea of Without Warning: Fight Back was born.

By asking questions in karate dojos, I learned that self-defense and karate are two different things. Karate relies on muscle memory and takes a lot of practice. I was looking for something

---

Your plan will increase your odds of surviving; it may buy you the moments you need to run to safety.

---

everyone could do, something simpler. I started working with the police department in a process of eliminating what was hard and making note of what was easy.

Now, through Without Warning: Fight Back, working with former police officers, I help others by teaching tools and tactics for awareness, attack-prevention and self-defense. We've filmed videos and developed a curriculum. We teach simple ways to prevent attacks based on real-life situations.

I learned from people in law enforcement that people who get attacked generally don't have a plan. A perpetrator has a plan—but he has just one plan, no Plan B. So, if you have a plan and you act, if you fight back, scream, make a scene, you've put him at a disadvantage. He won't be able to follow his plan and many times he'll just run away. Your plan will increase your odds of surviving; it may buy you the moments you need to run to safety.

Plans are best kept simple. For example, if you always hold your car keys in your fist with one of them poking out, you can hurt and startle someone who accosts you on the way to your car by just jabbing at him. Then you can run.

I learned that perpetrators feed on fear. Nowadays, when I give talks or classes, I can tell when people walk into the room who are most likely to become victims and who are least likely. I can tell by the way they walk, the way they carry themselves. You can increase your odds of avoiding an attack by walking with confidence—even if you have to fake it.

Whether it's Southern politeness or Midwestern nice, women are sometimes too polite for their own good. Instead of saying "Stop" when someone gets too close, they'll allow a stranger to get close enough to grab them. They wouldn't dream of screaming or making a fuss.

Right now, I'm working on a missing persons case. A twenty-year-old nursing student walked out of her house into her carport and, without warning, was abducted. She sent a text message at 7:41 a.m., as she was leaving the house. By 8:11 a.m. the police were at her house. So between 7:41 a.m. and 8:11 a.m., without warning, she was gone. The eyewitness stated that the woman was led away

Use your plan: Scream, make a scene, fight back.

from her house by a man in camo (thought to be her boyfriend). Who would think that we need a plan when we walk into the carport: *What would I do if I were attacked?* But we do need that plan; we need to put the odds on our side.

An attack happens in seconds. If we are able to call them, it takes police minutes to respond. Years ago, we were advised not to fight back. Now, though, police advise that we do fight back, raise a fuss. Above all, we should resist any effort to get us to go to another place—whether the attacker uses guile or force to try to get us to move. Don't go with him to the back of your car to see if you really have a flat. Don't go close to his car to give directions. Don't go with him to help him load an awkward package into his van.

And if he grabs you, scream, make a fuss, resist with all your might. Even if he's armed, it's better to be injured right there than to go with him to his lair.

In classes, especially in churches, we're often asked, "But we're supposed to turn the other cheek, as the Gospel says."

We tell the students, "While you turn the other cheek, they're going to stab you or take you to a secondary location. God does not want you to be tortured for three days until you beg to be killed."

For example, when an innocent homeless person asks for spare change, he keeps a respectable distance—he often is sitting down. When someone gets too close, gets right in your face, your internal alarm should go off and you should make a fuss.

We show pictures of good guys and bad guys in classes. It's amazing how many people say, "That one is a normal guy," and he is a mass murderer or a rapist.

You can't judge a person by the look. We also talk about indicators to look for that will increase your odds of avoiding an attack. For instance, if a man in a suit is wearing running shoes, be wary. If someone seems wrong, if something looks out of place, if the hair goes up on the back of your neck, trust your gut instinct—it is a God-given gift. Use your plan: Scream, make a scene, fight back.

You don't need two years of training in karate or tae kwon do. But you do need a plan. The police tell us that you have three seconds to respond effectively. That's just time enough to *do something*. And the simple things do work. We think of villains as somehow stronger than us, but if you think, "There's a coward trying to attack me," it empowers, emboldens you because you're dealing with someone who's inherently weak.

Nothing works all the time, but having a plan and acting on it can save you when you, without warning, find yourself in a dangerous situation. To give just one example, in class we told a group of female attorneys that the first thing to do is yell, "Stop."

Later, one of them told me how she had used that advice. She was in downtown Nashville walking to dinner. It was getting dark and the streets were empty. A man was approaching her.

"He wasn't going to ask me how I was doing," she told me. "I yelled, put my hand up and shouted 'Stop,' and he did." He was so startled that she had enough time to run away. She fought back and the odds shifted to her favor.

Someone asked me if, after the trial, when the beast who murdered Angie was tried and convicted, I had a sense of peace. No peace. There is no peace. I take the most horrific cases there are— rape, stalking, murder and missing persons. I work with families and with victims of terrible crimes. I am a better person working with them; they have strengthened me and led me to continue on. But I'm reminded every day of the tragedy that they've gone through, so there is no peace.

It is written: "A time for war, a time for peace." While people are being raped, stalked, abducted, murdered without warning, it is not a time for peace. It is a time to fight back.

Sheila Wysocki is a private investigator and founder of the non-profit Without Warning: Fight Back. Her life changing-story of how she helped solve the murder of her former roommate, Angie Samota, has been aired on a special Biography channel episode of I Solved A Murder *and on* Dateline. *She also was featured on* Live with Anderson Cooper. *In her classes, Sheila teaches awareness, prevention and training in defense tactics. Sheila uses her private investigator license to work on current cold cases including missing persons, rapes, stalkings and murders. She lives in Tennessee and has two children. Connect with Sheila at www.SheilaWysocki.com.*

Melanie Ware

Positively Adventurous

I wake up in the morning excited and anxious, wondering whether I'm about to have an amazing adventure or make the hugest mistake of my life. There is nothing in the house to eat and, questioning if eating something will give me energy or give me cramps, I get an egg sandwich and latte at the Starbucks on the corner and take some Advil® in hopes that it will take effect before the pain overtakes my body.

What was I thinking? I can't believe I am actually going to hike Grouse Mountain today. It's snowing; I don't own any hiking gear let alone snow gear and the last time I did a real hike, up Grouse Mountain coincidentally, was thirteen years ago. I just pray I don't end up another search and rescue victim on the six o'clock news.

I'd been dating Barry for only a few months and hadn't yet been hiking with him. For the last ten years, he had hiked Grouse Mountain every weekend, whether it was raining, sunny or snowing. He assured me that I was in good hands, but more than overcoming the treacherous weather conditions on the mountain, I was afraid he would discover that I was neither a "real" hiker nor "really" in shape and would break up with me.

When we arrive at the mountain base, I'm relieved to see that there is almost no snow. Maybe the trail conditions won't be as bad as I was expecting. As we head up the trail, the elevation gain gets steep very quickly, my heart races and my legs and lungs begin to burn. We are only about ten minutes in and already I can't breathe. My legs hurt and then I realize, *oh my God, I have at least two more hours of this.*

My thoughts race to having to be pulled up the mountain on that hike thirteen years ago and I panic, calling for Barry to come back. "Please stop! I can't do this. I'm sorry, but I'm just not ready for this."

"You've already completed the hardest part of the trail," he assures me gently, trying to calm me down. Although I know it's not true, his quiet confidence helps me to keep going. "You can conserve your energy if you focus on taking smaller steps and slowing your breath," he explains. I take his advice and follow his lead up the mountain.

As we climb higher up the mountain, the snow on the trail gets deeper and the snow flurries make visibility difficult. I continue to focus on the next step in front of me, which now is only the imprint of Barry's footsteps in the snow, keeping my breath and

---

I just pray I don't end up another search and rescue victim on the six o'clock news.

---

pace slow and easy. The trail is incredibly steep and, as I slip off the trail, Barry grabs hold of me with amazing speed and care, pulling me back onto the trail. Our hearts pounding, we catch our breath and hold tightly onto each other.

Stupid me, why am I wearing running shoes in all this snow? I realize that my focus, my faith and Barry are all I have to keep me safe. One slip and it will be game over. We continue our journey, staying close and maintaining one step at a time. As the trail becomes less steep, my fear subsides, and I realize how my faith in myself, my friendship and God has grown from this experience. My focus broadens to the quiet and beauty of my surroundings. The mountain's majesty and peacefulness remind me that my goal is more than just climbing to the summit, but also to find enjoyment in every aspect of my journey there.

As we approach the summit, our pace quickens as does my energy and excitement. Our arrival at the summit is met with complete exhilaration and overwhelming appreciation. *I did it!* I almost can't believe that I achieved my goal three months ahead of schedule. As we sit having a congratulatory hot coffee to warm ourselves, I think about the past year of my life and just how far I have come. Completing my goal of hiking Grouse Mountain was really just the "cherry on the top" of my life.

Only ten months earlier, I had moved back to my hometown in North Vancouver, British Columbia, Canada. Though I no longer had family or friends there, it still felt like home, and it brought me closer to my love of nature. My marriage of eleven years had ended the year before, and I was looking for a fresh start. My life and my health and well-being had been spiraling out of control for several years at that point; I was deeply depressed, a hundred pounds overweight and alone. Every part of me hurt and my emotions vacillated among hate for myself and my infertility, anger that my husband wanted to end our marriage and despair from my belief that everyone I loved and cared about in my life had abandoned me.

That first year, I hadn't been out of bed other than to go to work and walk the dog. Some days, my anger turned into complete rage only to be subsided by crying and desperation. I didn't understand why no one cared about me. I had always been there to take care of everyone else, fight for them and keep them safe. Didn't they know I needed help too?

I will never forget the day that changed my life. As I waited for the bus that day, I thought to myself that today would be a good day if I were to be hit by a bus. As I pondered that thought, I realized that I wasn't afraid to die. WOW! I was not afraid to die. What was I afraid of then? I was afraid to live.

That thought was not only my life changer, it was also my life saver! All day, I thought about the questions: *If I'm not afraid to die, why am I so afraid to live? Why am I so afraid to go after my dreams? If the worst thing that can happen is that I die, and I know I'm not afraid of that, why not go for it and do all the things I've always wanted to?*

I started taking back my life that day. My first step was a visit to my doctor's office to get help with my depression and the extreme pain in my body. My doctor wanted to prescribe anti-depressants, which I was afraid of. As a compromise, we agreed to a thirty-day

Our hearts pounding, we catch our breath and hold tightly onto each other.

challenge. I had thirty days to improve my depression with the help of exercise, nutrition and mindset; otherwise, my only choice would be medication. I was determined that was not the answer for me.

An "all-or-nothing" kind of girl who will usually rise to a challenge, it wasn't difficult for me to get started. Sustaining my new habits was what would be hard for me. This wouldn't be the first time I would overcome depression or lose weight and I knew I needed more than a thirty-day challenge if I was really going to reclaim my life.

As I walked home, I looked up at Grouse Mountain and knew immediately that it was my answer. I had my goal—by my birthday next year in June, I would hike Grouse Mountain. It was going to be a real challenge and I didn't know how, but I made the decision that I could do it. My life depended on it.

Grouse Mountain became my main focus and the catalyst for finding my purpose in life. I posted signs on my desk at work and around my house, stating the date I would hike Grouse Mountain, how many steps it would take and the elevation gain so that it would stay in the forefront of my mind. Every day, I looked up at that mountain while out walking and imagined myself climbing to the top. I then created a plan that incorporated small achievable changes to my diet and fitness regime.

I began reading personal development books that helped me begin changing my thoughts; got the support of a counselor to heal the wounds of my past; learned to regulate my insulin resistance and balance the hormone issues that resulted from premature menopause; and traded my job for a less stressful one so that I could focus my energy on myself.

For the first time in my life, I was taking care of me, learning to love me and make my own decisions.

As I loved and cared for myself, I learned to create boundaries and my compulsive need to take care of and be responsible for everyone else's needs and expectations somehow vanished. My transformation was incredible. I was almost unrecognizable inside and out. The extra weight released from my body effortlessly and I began to pursue things that I thought would only ever be dreams. I found the courage to build new friendships, salvage old relationships and to do things I hadn't even considered. The "real" me had come alive!

One week after achieving my Grouse Mountain goal, Barry and I head back to Grouse Mountain. Still excited by my achievement the week earlier, I'm determined to improve my time. About

---

The "real" me had come alive!

---

halfway up the mountain, Barry says, "You're going to be safe on your own from here. I want to go faster. Don't forget, just one step at a time. I'll see you at the top."

My heart races, my stomach sinks and as fear begins to set in, I remind myself of my success the previous week. As Barry disappears up the mountain, I continue to focus on one step at a time, and then I have a thought—*I'm alone and can set my own pace.* I alternate running the flats and walking with precision as the trail steepens. As I reach the summit, there's Barry with a surprised look on his face; I am only minutes behind him! Even better, I shaved thirty minutes from the previous week's time.

I discovered something very magical on that second hike up Grouse Mountain. The weather conditions were the same as the week before, as was my gear, and I am positive that I didn't get that much more fit in only one week. The magic was my belief in myself as a result of my having faith, finding my courage and gaining confidence from the success I had achieved by taking one small step at a time!

Melanie Ware is the founder of PositivelyAdventurous.com (PALS), a community that inspires women to live more adventurously and have the courage to love and express who they really are while fostering meaningful friendships. Melanie and her PALS are "Positive Adventurous Loving Spirits." Melanie's motto is "Learn, Grow and Share" and she considers herself a fledgling adventurer, explorer of life and authentic storyteller. You can't help but feel encouraged to "go for it" with Melanie's caring and compassionate guidance. You will discover that you are not alone and that anything is possible as Melanie takes you along on her journey through sharing fresh and endearing tales of her woes, mishaps and moments of success mixed with a little wisdom gained along the way. Together with Melanie and her PALS, life is more fun and definitely "Positively Adventurous!"

Visit www.PositivelyAdventurous.com to join Melanie and her PALS on their next adventure and learn how you too can live more adventurously with the courage to be and express who you really are through Melanie's blog and e-zine GO FOR IT – Your Guide to Living Positively Adventurous.

Kathleen Mundy

Stand in Your Name

Have you looked at your life and asked yourself, "How did I get here? Is this really my life?"

There are times when we find ourselves in a situation that is so far removed from what we expected reality to look like, we wonder how we could have travelled so far off course. It's as if we have forgotten not only our life plan, but who we really are. We compromise, and sacrifice, and do for others with no aim for own fulfillment. It's almost as if we have forgotten our own names.

Finding ourselves in a place of unrecognizable scope can be the best and longest-lasting motivator for change. Never mind how we got here—how can we continue on this path, and to what end?

I had my own "How did I get here?" moment when visiting my father in the hospital. He had been sick for some time, and when I looked at him, so pale and weak, I saw myself. I may not have been physically ill, but I was a shadow of my former self.

Growing up, I had loads of esteem. I had no problem taking bold steps and trying new things. What I did have a problem with was relationships. I had a pattern of getting involved with controlling men, which slowly chipped away at my healthy self-worth until I found myself willingly enduring the criticism, restrictive demands and humiliating taunts of my spouse.

Our friends thought we had everything—a big house, big cars, big money. But in reality, it was all a big lie. We started companies, hosted lavish parties, took exotic vacations and fought for control every day. We were together only months when the controlling behavior started and it got worse when our daughter Madison was born. Soon, my girlfriends stopped calling and dropping by.

My life was exclusively his. The negative comments and the arguing stripped me of who I once was. I still remember standing among friends at my thirty-sixth birthday party when he joked, "When she turns forty I'm trading her in for two twenty-year-olds." He was openly trying to shred what little self-esteem I had left. Although his comments that night were met by my nervous laughter, the threat of philandering ultimately turned into nightmarish reality.

By the time I walked into my dad's hospital room that day I was completely demoralized. I wanted to leave my relationship, but stayed because I gave in to his guilt trip about putting my three

*I may not have been physically ill, but
I was a shadow of my former self.*

children from my previous marriage through another divorce. I wanted to leave all of my children with a legacy and I had convinced myself that I had to stay married to do that. I started to believe I deserved the dark place I landed.

But I didn't share any of this with my dad. Instead I blurted out, "Why don't we go on vacation together?" I surprised both of us! Though we hadn't had a great relationship, I wanted to help him to find a reason to go on living, something to which he could look forward. And the truth was, I needed something to look forward to as well.

Dad didn't respond; he was a man of few words. But, when I came back the next day, he asked, "Where will we go?"

Not expecting him to want to go on vacation with me, or even ask where we might go if we did, again I blurted out the first thing that came to mind. I said, "Why don't we go to Ireland?" Again, he didn't respond.

When I came back the next day he asked, "When would we go?"

Having not planned any of this, I had no idea what to say. He hadn't said he would go yet, but he seemed delighted at the notion of it. So I replied, "We'll leave in June. But this is April, so you really have to get stronger if we're to make this happen."

My dad and I spent three weeks in Ireland. It was the best vacation I ever had. We laughed and we got lost; it was a tremendous experience. Time with my dad in that beautiful country gave me a

----

Our friends thought we had everything—a
big house, big cars, big money. But
in reality, it was all a big lie.

----

glimpse of the person I used to be, and what life was supposed to be like. And when he said, "I love you, Kathleen," I felt my heart begin to open and my mind begin to clear.

Two days after we returned from Ireland I visited with my eldest daughter and shared some of my revelations and insights. She said, "Mom, you have to make a change. You cannot go on living the way you've been living and there's no reason to do so."

I had encouraged my children to go their own way in life and test the challenges. Many times I told them, "If it feels right, move forward. If not, change course." Now, my children were echoing that message back to me.

My daughter went on to say, "Mom, you don't deserve to live like this."

In that moment I knew she was right. Her words carried me through the fear that had paralyzed me for so long and right then and there I made a plan to leave. Then I verbalized the plan, the entire process, until I was sure there was no going back. It was time to shift to a better life, a life with dignity, even if that meant I would have to start over with little or no income.

In the years after I left, I worked two jobs to keep us afloat. Madison worked forty hours a week through all four years of university.

One day, while looking for a commercial office building for a client, a fellow realtor said, "I don't have an office building, but I have a business for sale."

I said, "No, I don't think I can go down that road."

"You should look at it. It has a really healthy bottom line," he urged.

After looking at the business—a small pizza parlor—I knew it could facilitate what I needed. My dad was a blue collar guy his entire working life, so when he passed away, I was surprised to learn that he had left me a small inheritance—not a lot, but enough that maybe I could fund a small business, something to make life easier.

I realized that, in order for us to have more security and freedom, we needed to have control and this opportunity was just that. I also knew that one pizza parlor would help a little, but

In building and expanding a thriving business, I had also rebuilt my esteem.

because I couldn't work in the business full time, we needed more locations. It was time to give birth to luck and to shape our future.

Over the next five years, I self-funded the building of five more pizza parlors by minimizing what I extracted from the company until it grew to the point where it gave to me freely. I took a low wage and poured profits back into the company. When I couldn't get a bank loan for expansion, I went to second-hand stores and scoured through old used equipment; I built my business on a shoestring.

I knew I needed a solid, committed team to help me make my dream come true, so I provided my employees with extensive training, taught them about profit sharing, held quarterly meetings with my key employees so that they felt a sense of ownership and engaged my entire team in my goals for the businesses. I developed a culture of respect, working arm-in-arm with them if needed.

After the third store opened, Madison was offered a promotion at the job she'd been working at for four years and I said, "If you're prepared to work for another company, why don't you come work for me and we'll do this together?"

Five locations later, I realized that in building and expanding a thriving business, I had also rebuilt my esteem. It was as if I'd spent my whole life being called Jane, knowing all along that the name didn't fit, and then someone said, "Your name is Kathleen."

Success is not for the faint of heart.

Building my business *on my terms*—in gratitude; with a focus on substance, not flash; applying a calm, deliberate approach to growth—was like stepping into my true name.

When we're lost, or wonder how we ended up in this life that doesn't feel right, a life that depletes us, rather than fulfills us, we must take the first step toward remembering—or finding out—who we really are. Oftentimes, we figure this out through the process of making money. Let's face it—in today's society, money is our energy. Money helps us get the things we need, and it helps us help *other people* get the things they need. That's what fuels the big engine.

My devotion to helping women step into their own names through business comes from my own experience building back my self-esteem so that I not only recognized my life, I celebrated it. I believe finding yourself through business is the easiest thing in the world. It's brilliant because you have the control to own it, make it, tweak it, let it evolve and grow just the way you evolve and grow as a person.

You have more ability than you've ever dreamt possible. You have gifts that people need—all that you need is a vehicle to bring those gifts to the world. Entrepreneurialism is an opportunity to find your voice, to learn your name and take your message the people who are waiting for it. I'm just thrilled to death to be able to help guide women through this process.

The most critical aspect of making the initial shift is to understand you cannot do it alone. My first step toward building back my esteem was in taking a trip to Ireland with my father, and then leaning on my children and friends to help me leave a destructive relationship. I did not make these crucial changes alone.

Whether you get assistance from a voice through a video or audio, through the written word, or in person, you have to find it. But I think you know that already, otherwise this chapter wouldn't be speaking to you; otherwise you would have stopped reading on the first page.

Sometimes we lose sight of our own truth. We forget our own names, or we let others give us a different name, one that confines us, or keeps us from the path we were meant to walk, from joy and fulfillment. It happens to so many of us, even those of us who seem to have it all together—smart, accomplished, strong, confident, we are all capable of forgetting, of making compromises that slowly hack away at our self esteem until we are a shadow of our former selves.

Success is not for the faint of heart. I have found that success is bred through hard work, determination and an unwavering resistance to retreat. There is no room to flee; you are in the battle to win. The courage you need to succeed is deep within, rooted in your name, the truth of who you really are. Sometimes your name is buried so deep it can be difficult to see on your own. Accept the help of others; they have a vision, and together with your dream, you will find the courage to win.

One day you will stand in your own name, and rather than say, "How did I get here?" you will breathe deep, smile and say, "Look at this amazing life I've made." I know you will. I did. I know it's possible.

Kathleen Mundy is an author, entrepreneur and business coach who turned a small investment into a multi-million dollar business. Today, through her company, Making Your Own Money™, she teaches women how to reach their full potential and independence in the entrepreneurial world, and secure a better future.

Kathleen is the co-author of Reading Between the Wines *and is the author of* 7 Secret Questions to Making Your Own Money. *In 2013 she was nominated for an RBC Canadian Women Entrepreneur Award (CWEA). Connect with Kathleen at www.MakingYourOwnMoney.com.*

Kellie Poulsen-Grill

Happiness Is Mandatory

"Kellie, it's Dave. I'm stuck in bad five o'clock traffic on the I-5, it's pouring down rain and I thought I'd give you a call… how are you?"

At the sound of Dave's voice, my heart leapt. In many ways, I still felt like the moony-eyed twelve-year-old girl, crushing on her brother Brett's handsome best friend. Yet in the past two months, Dave had become so much more than a crush, so much more than a family friend.

When his beloved wife Teresa lost her battle with breast cancer, leaving him to raise their three children alone, Brett and I had flown up to Portland, Oregon to lend Dave support and attend the funeral. I was petrified—though I was a thirty-four-year-old professional songwriter who had had several boyfriends, somewhere inside of me was that young girl who scribbled "Kellie Poulsen-Grill" onto her school notebook, and I was concerned that my secret crush might not be a secret for much longer.

When Dave and his three darling, yet devastated, kids greeted us, I could feel my heart pounding in my throat. I knew instantly that even after more than two decades, I was *still* smitten with him. But I kept it to myself; I was careful not to act interested in Dave. Instead, I focused on helping his children. We clicked right away. Nikki, age fourteen, Lauren, age twelve, and Johnny, age ten, were a welcome distraction and I bonded with the three Grill kids on a level that to this day is difficult to explain. I took them horseback riding, bowling, swimming, to the mall—anything to keep them out of the way while Dave planned a celebration of Teresa's life.

After the well-attended funeral, I hugged the kids goodbye and we promised to write, email and call each other. Before I left, I turned to Dave and said, "If you ever want to write a song to help you deal with losing Teresa, I'd be happy to co-write it with you."

Dave had dabbled in songwriting and had even sent my twin sister Kaysie and I some of his songs a few years back. He was quite talented.

Life went on and, though the communication between the Grill kids and I was very strong, I hardly ever spoke to Dave. Then one December day Dave called me out of the blue. He said, "I have a song idea. I want to write about a pair of old cowboy boots—I married Teresa in them, and then I buried her while wearing them."

Fighting back tears I said, "That's an amazing idea, Dave." Within twenty minutes I had written our tribute song to Teresa and Dave's undying love for her.

There were a few more calls from Dave, and emails. Then, later that month, when Dave called to ask if he could gift his kids with

---

Dave had become so much more than a crush, so much more than a family friend.

---

a spring break trip out to Nashville to see me, I was so excited I agreed immediately. It was then that I realized, *I'm in love with all four of them!* Still, I kept it to myself. Dave and the kids were grieving, and I didn't want to interfere with their healing process.

Now, Dave was calling me just to talk on a cold and rainy day in the Pacific Northwest. I knew there was something blooming between us—could I let myself tell him the truth about my childhood crush on him—and my newfound love *for* him? Could

I let myself ask for what I wanted, even though some might feel I was moving too fast?

As Dave chatted away about the weather, I thought about the philosophy by which I had lived my life for as long as I could remember—that happiness is not optional. Happiness is not for the few, or the lucky, or for those who are "deserving." Happiness is mandatory, as important as air, as food and water. Happiness is our birthright.

And so, scared to death, I gathered my courage and said, "Dave, I have to confess something. I've had a crush on you for twenty-four years and… I'm in love with you and the kids." I held my breath, waiting for Dave to respond. Almost immediately

---

We both knew our lives would
never be the same.

---

he said, "I have to go," and shut down the conversation.

I was devastated and so mad at myself for taking the chance so soon after Teresa's death. I called my brother Brett and said, "I think I blew it with Dave. I'm such an idiot. What was I thinking?"

Before Brett could respond, my phone beeped to notify me I had a call waiting. It was Dave! Hands shaking, I clicked over and offered up a tentative "Hello."

Dave said, "I'm sorry I had to cut that short. Nikki got in the car so I could take her to voice lessons and I didn't want her to hear us talking. I'm free to talk now."

Heaving a giant sigh of relief, I calmed down and listened as Dave went on to tell me that he was flattered, and quite interested in what I had to say.

"I'm a realist, Kellie. I have three kids, and though I vowed to love her 'until death do us part,' I know I want to live and love again. Teresa made me promise that I would try."

"I've known you and your family for a quarter of a century—I know your ethics, and your morals and your character. I know your history," he continued. "The kids adore you! If there's a chance that this could possibly work, I want to try. I'm a forty-year-old father of three who didn't want my wife to die. I am going to date again and I'm very interested in that person being you."

My heart beat faster and I had the strangest sensation of my life just coming together, as if everything was exactly as it was meant to be.

We agreed to meet up on the Oregon coast in a couple of weeks. "We need to find out if I'm more to you than just Brett's friend and you are more to me than just Brett's little sister," Dave said. "I'm afraid that after all of these years I may not live up to your expectations. I may let you down, once you really get to know me."

Happiness is as mandatory as
air, food and water.

"Never!" I said. "I'll meet you anywhere!"

The moment we saw each other at Portland International Airport, we both knew our lives would never be the same. Our trip to Lincoln City was magic, complete with rainbows, pink sunsets and our favorite songs. We knew these rare experiences were signs from our angel, Teresa.

In December of that year, Dave, Nikki, Lauren and Johnny proposed to me and we were married the following April. I've been the "real" Kellie Poulsen-Grill for eleven wonderful years now. I adopted the kids, we raised our children, and now they have children. I live on a forty-acre horse ranch with the love of my life, my soul mate. Life is amazing and Dave and I are as madly in love today as we were on that day we reconnected on the Oregon coast twelve years ago.

If you don't ask, you don't get the reward. If I hadn't spoken up and told Dave how I felt about him and the kids, I am positive that I would have lost him to someone else. In order to have what we want in life we must step out on that ledge and jump. And the courage we need to make that leap comes from one essential, core belief, the same belief that helped me make the heartfelt confession that changed five lives: happiness is mandatory.

When we put ourselves in that mind frame—that happiness is as mandatory as air, food and water—we do not hesitate to go after what we want. We act boldly; we take chances. We pursue what we want; we easily remove ourselves from painful situations and unhealthy relationships; and we speak up for ourselves.

When we believe wholeheartedly that our happiness is mandatory, we don't fear negative outcomes; we *expect* a positive outcome. After all, our happiness is not up for debate. Why wouldn't life work out in our favor? Why wouldn't we find true love, fulfill our dreams and experience joy every day? If our happiness depends on the fulfillment of a desire, or a need, it will be so because our happiness is a given.

Research proves that we are all born happy little babies. As we grow up, our circumstances alter our natural happy state, causing us to become fearful, or unhappy, or to feel insecure and untrusting. We put our guards up and we start to believe that happiness is elusive, something reserved for the devout, or the fortunate, or the exceptionally worthy.

**Happiness is not something
you have to earn.**

Reclaim your birthright! When you know without a shadow of a doubt that your happiness is guaranteed, success is yours for the taking—no matter what the odds. Never, ever, *ever* give up on your dream. Whether it is a dream partner, a dream career, a dream house, or a dream family—go for it!

I lead "Success and Happiness" retreats at our beautiful ranch in eastern Oregon and we know full well the obstacles, roadblocks and challenges people face in the pursuit of their dreams. Love and life can be so unpredictable. Sometimes it can feel so defeating and so overwhelming; however, we must always believe in the impossible and we must always hold out for hope.

At our retreats, I teach the simple steps to accepting and applying the "happiness is mandatory" principle in your life. Follow these steps and you will start to see a marked change in your mood, and your good fortune:

Step One: Acknowledge that you were born happy. Everyone was born onto the same level playing field. Though our circumstances had a direct impact on our tendency to lean toward happiness—or not—we can go back to that base foundation of happiness. It is our *choice.*

Step Two: Make a conscious effort to find and read positive, uplifting stories and happiness affirmations on a daily basis.

Step Three: Every day, say this mantra out loud: "I choose to be happy today. I will be faced with challenges, but I will choose to stay positive and happy. Happiness is mandatory in my life!"

Step Four: Keep a gratitude journal. Each night, write out three things that went well that day, three things you are thankful for and three things that make you happy. At the end of each month, read through your entries. It will make you smile!

Step Five: Take risks. Even small attempts to get what we want out of life will help to reinforce the belief that happiness is mandatory.

Step Six: Stop associating with naysayers and negative people. No matter how happy you are, people who see the glass as "half empty" can bring you down. Their words can be toxic, so stay around positive, "half full" people.

Step Seven: Pray for guidance. Life is hard, and we can't go through it alone. Rely on your higher power to guide you, encourage you and support you in your journey toward making happiness a mandatory state of being.

Make the call. Confess your truth. Go after what you want knowing that your happiness is not something you have to earn;

it is something you were given from birth that can never be taken away.

Love is out there and it is perfect and meant to be. You can succeed against all odds in life and in love. Just keep the faith, believe and know that in life and in love there is always a plan. Let my magical love story serve as proof that your dream is your destiny, and it *will* come true!

Kellie Poulsen-Grill is a happiness expert, motivational speaker, author, songwriter and facilitator of her own "Happiness and Success" women's retreats held at her horse ranch in the majestic Pacific Northwest. She has studied and researched the effects of happiness and positive attitude for over twenty-eight years and shares her knowledge and unique insights in her work with people who want more happiness in life, and with employers who want happier, more productive employees.

Kellie is a proud member of the National Speakers Association and is Past President of the NSA-Oregon Chapter. She is the author of the audio book Happiness is Here: Simple Strategies for Staying Happy. *Kellie and her husband Dave co-authored the critically acclaimed non-fiction love story,* Send Me a Sign *with Doug Binder. Dave and Kellie own Whirlwind Publishing & Speaking Services (www. WhirlwindPublishing.com).*

Kellie and Dave live on Whirlwind Ranch in Wilsonville, Oregon, where they host transformational retreats for women (www. HappySuccessRetreats.com). They have three children and two granddaughters. Kellie is the Chairperson for the award-winning Oregon Horse Country. A portion from all of Kellie's happiness retreats, book sales and speeches goes to breast cancer research. Connect with Kellie at www.KellieSpeaksHappy.com.

Carmen Spagnola

Becoming a Channel
for Grace

There is never a time when the welfare office is empty. I had been sitting in my car for four days, waiting for a time when no one would see me go in, but now it was Friday, the end of the month, and with no hope of making my next rent check, humiliation couldn't keep me in the parking lot any longer.

Four days in a car is a lot of time for crying, so I was a puffy-eyed mess when I got to the counter. I was shaking with shame and couldn't look the woman in the eye; only a raw whisper made it past the constriction in my throat. "I don't know what to say... I'm not sure what I'm supposed to do here, exactly... but I am out of money and I can't get a job. Is there a piece of paper I should fill out?"

One look at me, and the lady got up, saying, "I am not supposed to do this, but you are breaking my heart." She took me straight to meet with a welfare officer.

I thought walking into that building was my lowest point, but I soon learned that, with barely two-hundred dollars to my name—including the coins in my pocket—I was still too "rich" for welfare. By this time I had learned how to stretch two-hundred dollars over a whole month, to cover most expenses for my five-year-old daughter and myself. But I still needed to pay rent somehow. For welfare to cover my rent, however, I was told I must return to the office on Monday with *less* than one-hundred-and-fifty dollars. I was crying again as I left the office. I felt as though I had nothing left in me—I had hit the limit of my capacity to endure. I never could have imagined this two years before.

In 2006, I'd had a spiritual vision: to open a high-end, ecological home furnishings store. At the time, I had a good job in sales but was living paycheck to paycheck. There was no way I could afford to finance my dream—it was crazy even to fantasize. Though I tried to clear my mind through meditation, visions of this store kept coming, so I saw a therapist.

She told me, "You're not going crazy; you're having a spiritual awakening. Let's do some regression therapy, and I bet it will be like flicking a light switch!"

She was right; thirty days later I had manifested a hundred thousand dollars in seed money and was standing in my

---

I had hit the limit of my capacity to endure.

---

stocked and staged retail store. One *year* later, our annual sales were nearly half a million dollars; I had appeared on Canadian Broadcasting Corporation (CBC) radio and the *Steven and Chris* television show and in *Canadian House & Home* magazine. I was speaking to audiences of twenty-five-hundred people at tradeshows, and appearing onstage at sustainability conferences with Ed Begley Jr., United Nations envoy Stephen Lewis, and head honchos from lululemon athletic wear.

And at the end of 2008, the economy went into palliative care and took my business along with it.

Suddenly, I found myself needing to declare bankruptcy. I was stunned. I couldn't believe it. In the space of a few short months, I had gone from strutting down the street to feeling so depressed I couldn't hold a conversation without welling up with tears.

I applied for every job I could, but even coffee shops turned me down—no one could match the accomplished person on my résumé with the soggy mess they saw in front of them.

For several months, I paid my rent by selling clothes and furniture on craigslist, but I couldn't afford to buy groceries. Desperate, I dug up part of the boulevard outside our apartment and grew kale and potatoes. Sometimes friends would visit and stock my fridge. I hadn't told them what I was going through—I was too embarrassed—they could just tell something wasn't quite right with me.

And now I had to *spend* fifty dollars to qualify for help. That was the most expensive fifty dollars I ever spent—it cost me another trip to the welfare office. That weekend, waiting for Monday to come, I hit the wall.

I had always had an intimate relationship with the Divine, spending time meditating and letting power and wisdom flow through me, but now that relationship was gone. I wasn't seeking God and not finding—I *had* found Spirit earlier in my life, I'd *had* that close bond, but now I'd lost it. I felt utterly bereft.

Over that weekend, I realized how mad I was. It seemed I had been calling and calling, and Spirit wasn't there for me. I'd lost

---

The light could only be found by loving things for what they were.

---

everything and now I was caught in this unending downward spiral. Lately I had even stopped meditating, because every time I sat on my tuffet I started to bawl.

Finally, I sat my butt down and just let it all drain out of me. I got mad, and I raged at the Universe, "Where are you now? What happened to unconditional love? Now that I really need you, where *are* you?"

The answer came back: "Why are you yelling? I'm right here! I've been here the whole time. Where were *you?*"

The answer froze me, gasping: I had trapped *myself* in this long, dark night. Long ago I had sworn to myself that, as an entrepreneur, I would never give up on my dreams or myself. Even if I failed. Even if no one else was there for me, I would be there for myself.

69

Instead I had been mean, critical and ashamed. My inner critic was merciless, my self-talk a never-ending loop of *Why can't you just get it together? How could you have been so stupid? What made you think you were so special you could make it big?*

"What happened to unconditional love?" was the wrong question to be asking of Spirit. I needed to look inside and ask, "What happened to unconditional love for myself?" Spirit flows through me, so how can it be there for me, if I am not there for myself?

I realized that I needed to face the truth of what had happened and accept the reality of the events that had led me to this point of clarity. But not only that; I needed to *embrace* the truth of my situation. "I made mistakes that led me to bankruptcy," I said

------

**You have to learn to love
yourself as Spirit does.**

------

aloud. "I was ego-tripping. I thought I was immune to what was happening in the world, that it wouldn't touch me."

It was the truth. I knew that I had to stop the running commentary; stop going over the what-ifs, the regret; stop trying to identify things I could have done differently. And most especially, stop blaming myself and Spirit. Darkness was behind me, and all around me; the light could only be found by loving things for what they were, incorporating them into my being and moving *forward*.

When I began to acknowledge and embrace the truths and parts of myself I'd been avoiding, I started to feel free in a way that I hadn't felt in a long time and doors began to open for me. When I talked openly about my struggles, people would often say, "I really needed to hear that." I had shared a part of myself that gave other people permission to be themselves and face their own truth. Listening to me speak about my own journey seemed to give them the permission they wouldn't give themselves.

In late 2012, I was asked to speak at a yoga conference. I was given seventy-five minutes to talk about the different stages of spiritual development. As I prepared my talk, I meditated, asking, *Please let me provide what these people need to hear. Please let me be fully in service to what they need.* At midnight, just hours before my talk, I received a new message to share, and wrote pages and pages of inspired work until two in the morning. I would have to read each word verbatim in order to fit the talk within the allotted time, but the next day I arrived at the conference early, feeling very calm.

And eight minutes before I was due to go onstage, I realized that all twenty-four pages of my speech were still sitting at home in my printer.

When I got up on stage, I said, "I prayed to be a channel for grace and to be in divine flow today, and now I'm going to have to be... because I've forgotten my speaking notes!" The last time I didn't know what to say, I was in the welfare office. This time, I just started talking—at first I was flustered and shaky, but I wasn't whispering. I began divulging my deepest, darkest story about the collapse of my business and having to declare bankruptcy. For the first time, I spoke of it without crying. I felt free—I was simply telling the truth.

As I completed my talk and came back into myself, I saw some members of the audience crying—and some of them were really bawling.

In that moment, I felt a real sense of my soul as embodied; my mind, body and soul were completely integrated. I felt connected with these people, who were clearly able to relate to my struggles. I thought they might relate to my message, and understand that if they weren't willing to go into the depths of their pain, they would only scrape the surface of their joy; growth is a matter of solving problems at the same level in which they are created, a matter of embracing and loving our own truth.

This is what Spirit does for us—it invites us to expand to new levels of empathy and awareness, and these new levels give us greater capacity to love generously, one soul to another. We must stop and face our truth, squarely and bravely—whether this journey begins in a welfare office, a doctor's waiting room, a college admissions office, a church basement or the arms of a friend.

At some point, you have to learn to love yourself as Spirit does, to have faith in your essence as the Universe does. You can't give up on yourself, or on the Divine. You illuminate your dark night by carrying your torch high, by being present for yourself, by not giving up on yourself, and by loving yourself enough to forgive yourself. In the dark night, we undertake the painful restructuring process of learning how to love and be loved, starting with ourselves.

Relish the dire agony of your situation. Love the aching inevitability that you will hurt and fail and be lonely and wretched, because that is precisely what is beautiful about life— the humanity of it, the universality of it. You will hurt, and I will hurt, no matter what we do; and therein lies our bond and our rescue. Our humanity is what makes us beautiful, and the Divine couldn't be Divine if we weren't human.

Stop wishing life to be different. Your truth is *yours,* and nobody can take it away, so give it a voice, embrace it—and surrender.

Through intuitive readings, past life regression and spiritual hypnotherapy, Carmen Spagnola helps people get clear on their life purpose and the next steps to living it. Part researcher, part practitioner, she takes a multi-disciplinary approach to spiritual development. Her work draws on depth psychology, the work of Joseph Campbell, Quakerism, feminist and aboriginal spirituality as well as developments in brain science and healing. Start embracing your own truth at www.CarmenSpagnola.com.

Janet Rickstrew

The Right Tools

Growing up a tomboy on a small farm in Colorado, I was encouraged to do all kinds of things to help out around the place—and what's more, I seemed to have a natural love and affinity for it. I followed my father around almost like a third son, never relegated to the kitchen or other "traditional women's duties," but rather learning how to fix fences, repair roofs, change tires and cut firewood with a chainsaw.

I was always willing to try anything that involved tools and projects, because I loved to fix things. There's such a feeling of accomplishment after you finish a project, stand back and say, "I did that!" That's what it's all about—not to mention the added bonus of money saved by using your own two hands, tools and expertise.

Years later, while attending a home party with a few friends in the late nineties, I realized—almost for the first time—that not everyone had had the same opportunities to learn this type of thing. My friends, watching me tinker and complete small projects around my house, would ask, "Can you do that for me?"

I wasn't interested in being a contractor or anything remotely close to it, but I *was* interested in teaching and giving other women confidence in this area. I thought, *What better format to teach and learn than in your own home, surrounded by your friends?*

After talking it over with a couple of friends, we came up with the business concept of teaching women basic home projects while providing them with better-fitting, ergonomic and easy-to-use tools. Once the idea began to take form, we set out to develop a friendlier line of tools for women. In conjunction with this, we would offer education through "Tool Parties." Our goal since day one has been to build confidence, inspire and empower women, and let them know that they don't always have to rely or wait for someone else to do a project. They *are* very capable, and can have a lot of fun in the process!

However, the first time we went "shopping" for tools at the annual National Hardware Show in Chicago, driving all the way from Denver, we got a big wake-up call about the industry we were trying to break into. Tens of thousands of people attend the hardware show every year, and it plays host to practically every tool company in the world as they sell to international corporations, large retail chains and local, independent stores.

My business partner, Mary Tatum, and I decided to attend the show because we thought it would be a fantastic way to find the companies we'd like to work with, not to mention an invaluable networking opportunity. Other than that, we didn't really know

---

We were actually told, "No, we don't have any interest in working with you."

---

what to expect—we were aware that hardware was a male-dominated industry, but many of our male friends had given our idea a positive response. So what did we have to lose?

Although we thought our idea was great, not everyone in the tool industry agreed. Some didn't understand why any changes would need to be made to their tools, and some had no idea why women would even want to undertake projects of their own. "After all, isn't that what husbands are for?" one even said, and although he laughed while saying it, it was obvious that he wasn't joking. Those were the more "polite" responses.

Many balked at our idea, chuckled behind our backs and provided us with sarcastic comments. The general attitude was, "You're entering into a man's industry, and we don't like it." It was disappointing and a little disgusting to see how we were shunned and turned away upon most inquiries. We were actually told, "No, we don't have any interest in working with you."

It wasn't until the third and last day of the show that we were able to generate even a modicum of interest in our idea and the service we were attempting to provide, when we came across a couple of salesmen who seemed interested in the idea. Each of them told us, "My wife would like this."

On the drive home, Mary and I both thought that perhaps our grand idea wasn't so grand after all. The challenge before us— breaking into a man's world while trying to build something that

---

"It's about time!"

---

had never been done before—looked far too daunting. Overcoming negative attitudes toward our idea was an extra obstacle we hadn't expected, and we began to realize that this business concept might very well not work out.

We regrouped and had a long, hard discussion about whether we wanted to move forward. "Is the initial belief and necessary commitment enough to overcome all the naysayers?" we asked ourselves. But there was a spark in both of us—and in our idea— that we both believed we could fan into a flame. Just because a few guys at a trade show told us no didn't mean the rest of the world would. We decided that our belief and our passion—coupled with the homework we'd now done—was enough, and made the decision to press forward.

Eventually, we met a few educated suppliers who could see the vision, and suddenly, we were on our way. Over the next two years, we slowly grew our line of tools in our online store, which also featured a "Tool Talk" area where customers could come to swap methods, expertise and success stories. It grew to be the most popular area of our site, though, since there was no room in our budget for marketing or media, it spread only through word of mouth.

In 2002, however, all that changed. *NBC Nightly News* approached us, wanting to do a story about us for Mother's Day, as they had noticed the growing trend in women wanting to work with tools. When the segment aired, we received so much web traffic—sixty thousand hits in the first twenty minutes following the East Coast time slot—that our server almost crashed!

That night, emails flooded in praising us for what we were doing and our business concept was finally validated. There really were thousands of women out there who wanted to learn more and become involved with Tomboy Tools because they loved the

---

I have two sets of tools, and only one of them is made up of hammers, drill bits and screwdrivers.

---

concept and wanted their own tools. The most common feedback we received through our website was, "It's about time!"

Two months later, we were featured in *Home Channel News*, an industry business-to-business magazine. The last time we'd attended and walked around in our logo t-shirts, we got some funny looks. Now, when people saw our shirts, we were stopped at least several times in each aisle by companies that wanted to supply us. "What a brilliant idea!" we heard, time and time again. What a difference two years can make! How quickly things can change and how quickly your idea can go from ridiculous to fantastic!

We have attended the National Hardware Show every year since, and one of the most encouraging things is the dramatic change we have seen in the industry. Each year we see more women in attendance, both as visitors and as representatives of tool companies.

Today—fourteen years later—we have a thriving business, with over two thousand sales consultants across the United States and

Canada, and we continue to inspire other women through our Tool Parties. Our goal of being the first company to offer education and top-quality, unique tools for women has been achieved. There is nothing more gratifying than putting a drill in the hand of someone who has never held or operated one and letting her try it. You can actually *see* a light bulb go off when a woman realizes how easy this can be and that she really *is* capable! She knows then that if she does a little homework and persists, she will be holding all the right tools.

The excitement and encouragement we receive from women all around North America is amazing. We never get tired of seeing and hearing how Tomboy Tools has been a blessing in their lives, from building their personal self-confidence and giving them a great set of "smarter" tools, to helping them earn extra income by sharing it with other women through the business opportunity we provide.

One of the most gratifying experiences came through a letter we received from a senior citizen living in New York City and trying to rebuild her home in the aftermath of Hurricane Sandy.

"I am one of the forgotten ones from Hurricane Sandy," she wrote. "I am self-sufficient, and have been rebuilding and fixing things all my life. I lost a lot in my small apartment due to the wind and water damage, and a lot of work needs to be accomplished, but I need help. I humbly ask for a set of tools and a drill as a hardship contribution from Tomboy Tools, and thank you for your consideration."

Identifying with her even more deeply than with our other customers, I felt compelled to help her. Against all odds—albeit, in a completely different way than we had done in the beginning—she was persisting.

I have two sets of tools, and only one of them is made up of hammers, drill bits and screwdrivers. The other is the stock I keep in doing my homework and persisting against even the loudest of naysayers. What projects could you accomplish, what could you build for yourself, if you equipped yourself with the right tools?

Janet Rickstrew is the CEO and co-founder of Tomboy Tools, a company that not only provides women with the tools they need, but also the education to use those tools. Janet has been overseeing the operations of Tomboy Tools for over ten years. She continues to enjoy "tomboy" pursuits, and can often be found tinkering around her home in Denver, Colorado, in her spare time. When she doesn't have a tool in her hand, she loves to enjoy the outdoors. From snowshoeing with her dog, Aspen, in the winter, to hiking with family and friends in the summer, she takes full advantage of the recreation that her Colorado lifestyle has to offer. Connect with Janet at www.TomboyTools.com.

Teri Jory, PhD

Poised for Greatness

My first true love was ice skating. Skates felt like an organic extension of my feet, and skating was a natural progression from walking. As a junior champion, I trained six-and-a-half hours per day, and there was nothing better than getting on the ice to warm up, skating as fast as I could around the ice and feeling the wind blowing my hair back. It was such a feeling of freedom and joy, like I couldn't be touched or stopped—as though I was a "superhero warrior."

After the warm-up from the laps around the rink, I would go to the side rail and shut my eyes, make myself breathe and focus on imagining the rest of my practice session. Then, I would do some core strengthening exercises of ballet barre and stretch my legs, hips and back to activate and isolate the muscles needed for a more focused part of my practice.

I knew becoming a champion would take more than going and skating every day, because some great skaters were much better than me, yet every time they would go into a competition they would fall. They just didn't have the consistency, and I would be the one who came out on top.

I knew, even back then, how important it was for me to meditate, think about my breathing and be connected to my body. Now, at the time in my life when I don't get out of bed in the morning until my body is centered, I know exactly what this routine at the side rail was—I was centering myself and making adjustments according to what my body told me. Mind you, nobody ever told me to do any of these warm-up techniques; I just intuitively knew to do them. I knew what made me perform best. As life went on, that routine of centering myself fell by the wayside; I didn't realize how dangerous this was until the unthinkable happened.

I was in Arizona, working as an award-winning television news anchor and health reporter, when one of my sources started stalking me. Several times, I reported sightings and death threats to the police, but as nothing had actually happened, they couldn't help me.

Eventually, however, the stalker took action. He broke into my apartment, held a gun to my head and told me that he was going to kill me.

He tied me up, beat me and then tried to strangle me to death. I was on my hands and knees and he had me in a chokehold with his fingers down my throat. It felt like a dream, I *wished* it was a dream, but I knew that it wasn't.

I could feel myself starting to get faint and lose consciousness, but I kept my mind focused thinking, *I will not allow myself to black*

He tied me up, beat me, and then tried to strangle me to death.

---

out and die at the hands of this man. I will not allow this man to kill me. I will survive, whatever it takes. My mom, family and friends would be heartbroken to think about the pain I had endured if I were to die and so my mind was in fast-forward, continuously thinking about every possible escape scenario.

All of a sudden, I thought of myself back at the side rail of my old skating rink, and I said to myself, *Connect to your body. Connect to your body, find that center and breathe.* In my mind, I went through my fingertips, wrists, arms, shoulders, my entire body until I got to the core. My body went into "superhero warrior" mode; I gathered up every last drop of power I had inside my soul and managed to break away.

I called the police from a neighbor's house while the stalker stole my car and took off. A police chase ensued into a very populated area, where he started threatening to kill other people—but the police ended up killing him. The nightmarish time I'd been experiencing at the hands of this man, through both the threats and the attack itself, was finally over.

The woman from a women's shelter who came to my assistance stayed by my side, holding my hand and telling me over and over again, "What happened is not your fault. Stay poised, just stay poised."

At that point, I knew that I could either roll over and let my heart and soul die or I could persevere. I was aware not only that

---

I could either roll over and let my heart and soul die or I could persevere.

I would never be the same person I was before this horrendous incident, but that I could grow from it, somehow. I realized that mental and physical astuteness were the life forces that kept me alive. But where did all that strength come from when I was near unconsciousness? If you'd have asked me before this happened what I would do in such a situation, I would not have been able to answer.

It wasn't until later, when I was recounting the experience in my journal, my safe place to release my emotions, that I realized exactly what I had done. *Wow! I could have lost my life right there, but I connected. I did it.* In the moment of being captured and almost killed by a six-foot, three-inch man, I experienced, and then realized, the true ultimate power inside that drives one's determination into action.

I was spurred to move in a new direction. Ballet and pilates had been huge pieces of my figure skating champion puzzle and continued to be prominent in my life as a professional ice skater, dancer and choreographer, but now was the time for something that would help me focus and center my body in a completely different way—martial arts.

Martial arts helped me to truly realize and focus my power source inside and become a new person: a fourth-degree black belt and an experienced warrior—as opposed to a survivor—with an empowered and lively heart and soul.

It wasn't until I gained eighty pounds through a tough pregnancy that I found my true purpose. After giving birth to twins, I struggled to find enough time and the proper technique to get my body back into shape. Sheer determination was my guide: I relied on my past athletic training and began to experiment in combining moves from ballet, pilates and martial arts. My body quickly responded to the new regimen, toning, sculpting and ultimately shedding the weight I'd gained.

My friends started asking me what I was doing and I showed them—and then their friends started asking them what they were doing.

I was so busy and suddenly all these people were begging me, "You have to find the time to teach us, *please.*"

And I thought, *Wow. They get it; I can do this.* Although what I went through was anyone's worst nightmare, it gave way to a new compassion in me, and the more I thought about it, the more the words of the lady from the women's shelter came back to me: "Stay poised."

I had to deconstruct my techniques back to basics, because I realized that not everybody else could do what I could already do with my body. I had to make it simple, so that everybody could understand it. The clients I coached were finally able to succeed in their goals and it all came from the body—and not all of their goals were fitness goals. Some of them were just regular life goals that they could now achieve because they were approaching them from a place of being centered and attuned.

We go through life and wear our stressful experiences and, through doing what is expected of us, we lose our true selves. A lot of us don't think, "I'm so confident." Instead, we think, "I'm not sure this is what I want to do, but I don't know if I can do anything else." You have to have a safe place. You need that to be able to let go, to be able to connect with yourself and let your real emotions shine through and your safe place should be you, at one with your core. You should wake up every day, put that energy in your core, feel the power and get up, saying, "Now, what am I going to accomplish today?"

When you come from your center and you're connected to your body, seeing from inside out and not seeing outside in—meaning what other people are seeing of us or what's expected of us—that is when you can achieve your goals. Seeing from the inside out makes everything clear, like the difference between high-definition and regular television, but it takes effort. You have to first of all work on yourself to constantly find that center; every day that center might be a little different because you had a divergent experience the day before, but you will still find it.

Being so much more connected with myself, I started going after my own long-held dreams, one of which was ice skating outside in the park. When I moved to New York, I knew it was my chance to make that dream come true. Wintertime came; I grabbed my ice skates and went to Bryant Park for the greatest New York experience ever! I got to encounter my first love, ice skating,

---

We can all be superheroes in our own lifestyles.

---

outside. It was snowing and I felt like I was in a snow globe, the only one alive.

I was truly living my dream; I was that "superhero warrior" once more. As I started out skating laps around the rink, going as fast as I could. I felt the freedom, but I also felt a new awareness of my body that I hadn't felt before. *Can this really be happening?* I wondered. I kept going through my regular training routine, and yes, it was true—I was actually better than I was before. I could fly as high as I wanted to because my body was so much stronger and knowledgeable about where my posture needed to be placed. Fascinated by this revelation, I couldn't get enough, and I was even more inspired to share with the world that we can all be superheroes in our own lifestyles.

From my experience with the attack and from coaching many clients, I know now that every one of us has an abundance of power inside; that most of us are only using a fraction of the mental and physical power within us, skimming only the tip of the iceberg. I was determined to not let my perpetrator win during the capture, and he didn't. What are you determined to do or not do in your life? What *could* you do if you were coming from your center?

Dr. Teri Jory, PhD, is an A.C.E. (American Council on Exercise) personal trainer and life coach, a fourth-degree black belt in Tang-Soo-Do martial arts, a professional dancer and choreographer and a figure skating champion/ judge. Her revolutionary POISE fitness technique has won many awards and has changed the lives of thousands of women across the world. Find your center at www.PoiseProductions. com.

Wendy Rice, PsyD

More Than One Thing

After a difficult delivery, sweet Wendy, the third child after two boys, was born with a droopy right side. The doctor said I might not be able to run and do other physical activities like normal kids. However, by the time I was three, I was whooshing down the mountain at "Snow Bowl" in New Jersey and slipping, sliding and gliding around on my little white figure skates. I seemed to have overcome the birth issues just fine.

As a little kid, I constantly lost things and was forever having to clean up my mess. My brothers and I often spent weekends skiing with my dad and there was never a weekend when I didn't lose a hat, a mitten or a pair of goggles. At home, I loved my pretty blue and yellow room with the matching wallpaper and bedding and windows that let in lots of light—it never lost that clean, new smell. But, most of the time, I just couldn't manage to hang up my clean clothes, get the dirty clothes to the hamper or even see the top of my desk. It wasn't that I didn't want to; I did, desperately. I so wanted to be responsible and organized.

My best friend, Amy, and I were in the same class in second and third grade. We shared our love of reading and both had curly brown hair. We spent so much time together that people often confused our identities—one year we even got buttons that said, "I'm Wendy, not Amy" and vice versa. School came more easily to

Amy. I thought it was hard and I wondered why. People said I was smart, but my memory was about the size of a flea, and I struggled to grasp both the big picture AND the little details. My inability to figure how things fit in order, how they related to each other, dates, spelling, rules—all of this made school incredibly confusing. I often didn't even understand enough to know what questions to ask. I was sure I was the only one who didn't get it.

In an effort to protect me from feeling inferior, my mother requested that Amy and I be placed in separate classrooms for fourth grade. I felt as though I was a complete moron.

That summer, for eight weeks I went to sleep-away camp, where they had a riding program. I would do anything to be near the horses, to be at the barn, immersed in that comforting, delicious smell—shavings, hay, sweat, saddle soap, herbivore poop. I had always loved animals passionately—I was drawn to the petting zoo, the cat that lived under the neighbors' porch, any stray dog. Animals always came to me and, though I was never antisocial, I found them much easier to hang out with than some people. But I had never had a pet. On visiting day, I begged and begged my parents to let me take three introductory riding lessons.

My horse was named "Willing," a sweet golden palomino; our first lessons together were in a small ring on a lunge line, going around in a circle like a tetherball. That was the beginning of the end. I just loved it.

I was in my element. I didn't feel so incapable with horses; I just felt love. I could groom them, handle a pitchfork, clean a saddle and, after a while, I could tack up a horse properly. I was never well organized; I was (and remain) the girl who got on my horse, felt my head and realized, *Oops, I forgot my helmet! Oops, these are two right-handed gloves!* Sure, I'd have anxiety dreams, such as being unable to get my horse over the jumps, but I loved riding so much I just pushed through my fear.

More than anything, I loved just being with the horses, breathing with them, intuiting how they were feeling by watching their ears, their facial expressions or how they were standing. *When a horse gets scared,* I noticed, *sometimes it runs away—but sometimes it will get BIG, like a dog with its hackles up. Sometimes it will turn into a fire-breathing dragon.*

Being able to be still and be patient and understand that there were hot horses, and quiet horses, and shy horses, skittish ones and brave ones, arrogant and obnoxious ones, I became a very good observer of body language. I knew who was ticklish, who would easily lift their foot up, who wanted me to breathe into their nostril and love them up.

As I struggled with high school, family issues, normal teenage stuff AND feeling stupid and incompetent much of the time, I became terribly depressed, irritable, anxious and withdrawn. I felt so horrible about myself, I wanted to die. *I'll never be able to write this essay, understand this class, pass this test.* I had a pact with a

---

I felt as though I was a complete moron.

---

fellow struggler: Neither of us was allowed to kill herself without calling the other first.

What saved me was being at the barn with the horses, a "think outside the box" school schedule and a wonderful therapist. With the right dose of an anti-depressant and lots of support, somehow I stayed alive, graduated from high school and was even accepted into college. To this day, I maintain that my induction into Phi Beta Kappa was due to my college having to admit a certain number of students, not to my academic performance! Alas for my self-esteem, one of the first things I heard in grad school from a professor was, "A person's vocabulary is the best indicator of his intelligence." *Great, just great! Great. Nice confirmation of my stupidity!*

Stupid as I thought I was, I managed to get through grad school and pass the national psychology licensing exam. And for some inexplicable reason, I found myself intrigued with testing and diagnosing learning disabilities. (Gee—I wonder why?) I was a whiz at talking about cases and test results, but the science part still stumped me. I could talk through a huge battery of test results and really get it, but writing it up was like running a marathon! *What the hell is the matter with me?*

Then, in a postdoctoral program about clinical neuropsychology, I finally put the pieces together: *The right side of the body is (mostly) controlled by the left side of the brain. Verbal memory and language function are largely located in the left side. The structures responsible for attention, prioritizing, starting, organization and planning are vulnerable to oxygen loss.* My difficult delivery, which everyone

---

You don't have to be smart in every way to be really good at what you do.

---

thought might have physical consequences, had a much deeper—albeit more subtle—impact. *I'M NOT A MORON!*

While other people always told me I was smart, I never believed it. How could I be smart and so stupid? I couldn't play Trivial Pursuit, since regurgitating facts was not my thing. I couldn't keep my papers organized for more than ten minutes and my reading comprehension left much to be desired! But when I put the birth injury pieces together and realized that it really, really wasn't my fault, I also realized that I had at least one great skill: I could intuitively understand people and their problems, just as I'd always done with horses.

I could find ways to phrase conceptually complex and emotionally difficult information in a way that it could be heard. I could "sell" or convey my understanding with solid facts to support it. I finally got confirmation from other people whom I deeply respected for their intelligence that I had real gifts as a psychologist. Wow! I began to recognize that you don't have to be smart in every way to be really good at what you do.

My amazing therapist in high school, and those who have followed, never judged me and worked so hard to understand and help me through my misery. Their empathy and compassion left an indelible mark on me and became a gift I am passionate about giving to others. Because I get learning, memory, attention and even emotional difficulties from the inside out, I have an uncanny ability to understand and explain those problems to those who also experience them. That synergy, that connection, is what it's all about for me. When I can give people the gift of feeling understood and loved for who they are, I go home happy. When people say, "Yes, you've got it!" then I have a shot at helping them.

Having learning, attention, memory or even severe physical or emotional problems is not the end all and be all; they do not have to define you. Chances are you probably have as many strengths as you do weaknesses. So even if you're awful at some stuff, know what that is, know what you're good at and don't let the things you are bad at stop you! Get as much help as you possibly can to understand your unique gifts and challenges. Everyone's brain is different and that is a wonderful thing.

If a client of mine has a challenge, we figure out what it is and name it. I was talking to somebody recently who said, "I've always thought of myself as just lazy and lacking willpower." Well, you could think of it that way OR you could say, "Task initiation is difficult for me. And sometimes it's hard to persevere in the face of distractions or when I'm tired."

You can take steps to deal with this issue, such as making a list of ten things to do in order to make getting started on a

---

Everyone's brain is different and that is a wonderful thing.

---

difficult task easier. Is there a way to take some of the challenges out of the equation? Can you get support for them? Modify your expectations around them? Labeling yourself—like me calling myself a moron—is a mind trap. You're just throwing the baby out with the bathwater: "What's the point of doing anything, I'm just lazy." Your perceived weakness becomes all-encompassing, as opposed to, "Part of my personality is: It's hard for me to get started on things that seem difficult."

Once, I labeled myself "stupid." Now, I can honestly say I'm phenomenally good at SOME things. Nothing wrong with that! When people listen to me talk, either in my office or when speaking in front of a larger audience, they often assume, "She's not like me." But lo and behold—I'm more like you than you realize. I just have many, many systems in place to help me make lemonade out of my lemons. I continually try not to beat myself up for the things I'm not so good at, give myself props for what I'm awesome at and surround myself with smart people who have strengths where I may not.

These days, I have the most wonderful horse named Sherman, a big, gentle good egg who doesn't spook easily and always gets us to the other side of the jump. We've been together for three years. And even though I still sometimes have challenges memorizing new jumping courses and believing in my abilities, I've learned that that doesn't make me a moron. I simply have to pay a different kind of attention, repeat the course back to my trainer, create associations with the different jumps to help me remember the order and trust that I have what it takes to find a comfortable take-off distance to each jump.

Being compassionate toward myself about how I process information, how I learn and how I remember makes me kinder and more patient with my horses and with other people, too.

In order to do therapy, in order to ride a horse, in order to do anything you care about, you have to have a sense of mastery and ownership of your skills, a belief that you can do it. I'm finally developing that belief: I have a good core skill set; I have muscle memory and instinct. If things don't go right today, it's okay. Maybe I need to lower the fences a little today, knowing that once I feel confident I'll be able to go back to my normal jumping height. I rely on my skills, believe in myself and believe in my horse—we're together in this, and when we let go, we fly.

Originally from New York, Dr. Wendy Rice has managed to combine her love of kids, animals and psychology into a wonderful life in Tampa, Florida. She earned a BA at Skidmore College and her master's and doctoral degrees in psychology at Yeshiva University and completed postdoctoral programs in psychodynamic psychotherapy and in clinical neuropsychology. Dr. Rice moved to Tampa in 2001 and opened her solo private psychology practice. Since that time, she has become widely known and sought after in the Tampa Bay region as a highly qualified, compassionate and straightforward psychologist for children, adolescents and adults, providing consultation, testing and assessment, therapy and innovative treatments to help a wide variety of emotional, behavioral, learning and relationship problems. In 2010, she created Rice Psychology Group, which currently has several licensed psychologists, certified coaches and therapy dogs in two office locations. Connect with Dr. Rice at www.RicePsychology.com.

Gorana Angert

Being Okay, No Matter What

"Don't go to class tonight."

The voice seemed to come from out of nowhere, as I was observing my Friday ritual of getting a manicure before my seven p.m. Brazilian jiu-jitsu class. I was waiting for my nails to dry, and suddenly I was taken over by the feeling that I shouldn't go to training. I had been training since 2008 and had loved it from the start, so much so that I made a point of never missing a class.

"I'm just down the street. It would be silly not to go," I told the voice dismissively.

As I entered the dojo building, the voice piped up again, and once more I dismissed it—I took pride in the commitment I made to my training and wasn't about to be warned off by some imaginary voice in my head. I was already in the building, and I wasn't going to just turn around and walk out. I donned my gi and stepped onto the mat.

The voice said, "You shouldn't be here tonight."

I ignored it, proceeded through the warm-up and soon enough was sparring with a classmate. I fell during the very first move, landing on my left shoulder and crying out from the sharp flare of pain. I stopped to check my shoulder; though the bones and muscles felt as though they were where they should be, I felt the blood drain from my face, leaving me white as a sheet. The classmate with whom I had been sparring brought me a bottle of water, and I watched the rest of the class from the side of the mat.

At the end of class, I shrugged off everyone's concerned inquiries about how I was and whether they could do anything for me, saying that it was probably a sprain and that I would be fine. On the drive home, all I could think about was how stupid I was

---

The voice said, "You shouldn't be here tonight."

---

for not listening to my intuition and getting hurt as a result. But, as a positive and optimistic person, I always hope for the best, and I figured it would be okay—particularly after having talked to my instructor, who had had the same injury, which had turned out to be a sprain—and everything was fine until I got home.

It was a dark, cold January night, and almost as soon as I stepped out of the car, I slipped on ice and fell. *Darn,* I thought, getting back to my feet and making my way inside, all the while telling myself: *No problem. I am fine.*

But then I saw the bump on my clavicle. It turned out to be clinically broken, which only really served as confirmation of what I already knew. The first thing that went through my head was, *How long will I be off the mat?*

My twenty years of studying mind-over-matter techniques prepared me well for managing the pain, and actually I wasn't in pain at all. I was simply angry with myself.

The next week was a blur, as I went about my business while waiting for surgery to repair my broken clavicle, which had, in fact, snapped in half. It took one skilled surgeon, one stainless steel plate, six screws and approximately forty-thousand dollars to fix. It was only afterward that my punishment truly began: The prognosis was that I must stay away from the mat for three months.

Three months? I thought. *No way. I can and will be back on the mat sooner than that.* I used everything I knew about how the mind works to heal my bone so that I could go back to training. I meditated, took supplements and used some Jedi mind tricks. For two hours each and every day, I imagined my surgeon telling me that I could go back. I visualized sitting in the room at my two-month checkup, picturing every detail, right down to the doctor's light blue dress shirt beneath his white coat and the chair on which I would sit—next to the doctor's table, and not where people who were actually sick would lie.

Most of all, I pictured the puzzled look on his face when he looked at my x-rays and told me that he had never seen anything like it, that my bone had healed so much earlier than expected. I listened for the exact pitch and intonation of his voice when he would tell me that I was finally free. And he did. It happened exactly the way I knew it would. I was free.

When I went back to class the next week, it felt like taking a deep breath again. I was finally able to get back to the thing I loved most! My classmates were happy to see me, and I was happy to be back. But as a few training sessions passed, I came to realize that

---

I stopped judging myself and
remembered my own life philosophy:
"I'm okay, no matter what."

---

while I had been healing, they had been making leaps and bounds in their progress. I felt left behind, that I wasn't as good anymore, that I had forgotten every move I knew. I just couldn't feel it. It wasn't the same, and I was frustrated.

When I asked my instructor for some extra guidance, he was happy to help me and kind enough to offer me some private lessons. I showed up to each and every one. One Saturday morning, we practiced together for an hour, mostly limiting the boundaries to playful sparring, but I couldn't do anything. Every move I tried was blocked, or turned back against me. I was getting choked left and right. I would tap, but continue to persevere, grateful for the extra time and help I was being afforded.

After our session, I slouched into one of the chairs in front of the mat, sipping my coconut water. My gi was soaked and disheveled; I was covered in sweat with my hair a mess, and I felt completely on edge. *What just happened?*

My thoughts were a flurry, as if my mind was a snow globe someone had come along and repeatedly shaken, over and over and over.

I am just not good enough. I can't hack this. Everyone is better than me. I don't know enough. I missed too much. I sat there looking at my painted toes, completely demoralized. Obviously, this wasn't for me, and I was ready to quit.

The ultimate leverage is in understanding that you are never at risk.

Unable to move, I sat still, breathing and observing the thoughts as they came and went, one by one, each one worse than the last. I needed to let the snow globe settle. And as it did, clarity emerged. I stopped judging myself and remembered my own life philosophy: "I'm okay, no matter what."

Jiu-jitsu is designed for a smaller person to defend against a larger, more powerful opponent in a situation where there are no rules or time limits. To be successful, you must be able to think two moves ahead calmly and clearly, even while your opponent is choking you or breaking your limbs. In other words, you have to be comfortable in a worst-case scenario, and in doing so, you eliminate the worst-case scenario. You are okay, no matter what happens. Somewhere along the way I had lost sight of that.

Sitting on that chair and watching the snowflakes settle as I sipped my water was a turning point for me. In that moment, I realized that my injury had been a minor one, and that I had made a big deal out of it for no reason.

We create our own experiences based on the thoughts we focus on, the meanings we assign to them and the actions we take. We can let ourselves become derailed completely by the weight we give to things that don't need to be weighing us down, both in our personal and professional lives.

You don't necessarily need a huge life obstacle to overcome in order to be okay no matter what. All you need is the knowledge that in life and in business, there are wins and there are losses. It's when we get stuck on the losses and attach too much meaning to them that the leaps we must take start seeming too risky, and we never make the jump.

The ultimate leverage is in understanding that you are never at risk. The real you, the formless you is never at risk. Your body, your finances, your revenue, even your pride may be at risk. But *you* are never at risk.

People play differently when there's nothing at risk. How would your game change if you knew you would be okay no matter what?

Gorana Angert is the founder of the Ultimate Scenario Company and helps entrepreneurs to honestly express themselves through their business using video technology to effectively tell their stories. She holds a blue belt in jiu-jitsu, a black belt in karate and a certified strategic interventionist qualification from Robbins Madanes Center for Strategic Intervention. You can connect with Gorana at www. UltimateScenario.com.

Karen Leckie

Leap Beyond the Possible

My teeth chatter in the cold morning water of the resort lake in Ontario, Canada—either from the chill or in stark terror. My coach, Randee, is telling me to keep my core tight, buttocks tucked in and shoulders back. But, I hear what has been my life's mantra for too many years, permeating every activity I tried, in business and in life: *I can't do it; I can't do it.*

My worst fear is that my left leg will take all the weight and my right leg will collapse, leaving me completely imbalanced and tied up like a pretzel in the middle of the lake. *If only I'd never had that car accident twenty-one years ago.*

In 1991, while I was studying engineering in college, I was in a car accident that crushed the foundation of my body and simultaneously crushed the entire foundation of my life. A broken pelvis and sacral bone left me with nerve damage in my right leg. To this day, if I'm stressed out, or if I do anything that imbalances me at all, if I walk the wrong way, or sometimes if I just walk on hard surfaces for ten minutes in a mall, I'll have pain for about three days. I'm scared to push myself, because I think as soon as I push myself, I'll be in pain. Because my right leg doesn't have full function, my left leg overcompensates and hurts.

It takes an emotional toll too. Since people can't see what's wrong, they can't understand my struggles. I can't wear high heels, so I can't dress up the way I'd like to present myself. I've felt "less than," not "normal," left out and inferior to everyone else.

My life has had its share of upheavals. I left engineering and became a teacher. In my last three years of teaching, I co-created an innovative self-directed learning program called jPod together with my former principal, Nancy. When that ended, I left teaching to become an entrepreneur. In 2005, my parents' marriage dissolved and my mother became very sick with a lung condition. She remained very sick for three years and passed away in 2008. My world completely collapsed around me with the anchor and cornerstone of my life, my mother, being gone in physical form. I became so despondent that I would sit for hours on the couch in my living room, expecting her to walk through the doorway at any moment.

Exactly six months later, in May 2009, I was diagnosed with breast cancer. It was a personal tsunami, the kind that wipes away all that you have ever known before and leaves you no choice but to rebuild. The only way to move is forward, and all the old rules no longer apply. I spent three years on a spiritual quest, flying to Peru and Brazil to figure out my life purpose. *I have never "just been me." I have always lived my life under someone else's prescribed*

I'm scared to push myself, because I think as soon as I push myself, I'll be in pain.

---

boundaries and unconscious conditioning. I went deep inside on my spiritual quest, gathering strength and coming in touch with my authentic self. In the end, I was stronger, physically, mentally and emotionally and now had the support in my life to take on the next challenge.

I had learned to know myself beyond the limitations of my own mind. Knowing yourself beyond the limitations of your own mind means seeing yourself beyond your own self-imposed restrictions. We have restrictions on ourselves, and we don't ever question them. We don't think we can go beyond them until we're placed in a situation where we actually see ourselves go beyond them—then we have to reevaluate what we think is possible for ourselves.

Coaches always say that the thing that makes your knees buckle is the thing you should do first. Get it out of the way. Go outside your comfort zone and really take a leap beyond what you think is possible.

Waterskiing makes my knees buckle. It is related to my body, but it is also a metaphor for my mind and my emotions and what I thought I was capable of doing. So here I am, quaking in my life

---

**The thing that makes your knees buckle
is the thing you should do first.**

---

jacket, waiting for the boat to come around yet again. *I can't do it; I can't do it. I can't possibly do it.* A few more failed passes and I am still bobbing along in the lake, breathless and anxious, wasting precious energy on fear rather than building up the courage to handle the next go.

Then I see Randee coming down the dock with a new contraption, a type of sit-down water ski attachment. Randee's father is driving the boat, coming around for a pass.

At that moment, I decide that I will not do the sit-down version. *I will stand up on my own two feet!* I can hear my coach Rich: "Just let it all go, don't think, just do." That is the only way to get out of your comfort zone. Take action; you can't read a book and learn how to do. The only way is to just do. And I do. I grab the tow rope. It tightens and I am off! The muscles in my thighs hold me up. I am standing, holding the rope. Jubilation! Effortlessly, I glide around two full tracks of the entire lake. I have leapt way beyond what I thought was possible. That leap totally changed my self-image. I had to rewrite my own history.

Wow! If this is possible, then what is possible in other areas of my life where I've been holding myself back? I had to just start from scratch and examine everything. From what had been my greatest weakness, I had derived my greatest strength.

I approach things now with the beginner mindset; I try not to have preconceived notions of what I think is possible in life or in business and just have no fear. I just let go and do, with a clear mind, with no prejudgments, no restrictions, and just see what's possible, because I literally don't know what is impossible. I might be able to do something that others think is impossible, just because I don't know it isn't possible.

Because I don't know that anything is impossible, every day is a new opportunity. Every day, we get to create something new. There are so many possibilities; I can try to live into my full potential

---

Because I don't know that anything is impossible, every day is a new opportunity.

---

rather than holding myself back and thinking only "normal" people can do this or that. Maybe I can do things that others wouldn't even try, and maybe I'll even surprise myself.

As a coach, I've seen that many start-up entrepreneurs have a lot of doubts about themselves. They might have had a lot of messages from others who said, "You can't start a business. Who says you can make money from living your passion? Who says you can do that?" People who have been employees have a lot of doubts, because it is so hard to go into the marketplace with your own work. Taking one knee-buckling leap beyond the possible, just letting go and doing it, helps them trust in themselves and believe in themselves that they are worth it.

For example, a few of my coaching clients were hanging onto other jobs at the same time they were trying to launch their real passions. They just didn't believe it was possible to actually earn a living from what they really wanted to do. I help them take the leap, fully letting go and saying, "I can earn a living with my whole life's purpose, life's mission, my blessing that I've been given by God."

Take your own leap beyond what you know is possible. Visualize yourself in a new activity, one that right now you don't believe you can do, and then think of the best-case scenario. Think of the best case of every single detail for two or three minutes at the beginning and end of every day. You'll usually start to see a shift right away if you do it with full feeling and are totally experiencing it, but since it takes twenty-one days to change a habit, the shift will probably take twenty-one days to become permanently ingrained as a new state of mind.

When I am waterskiing, I can totally let go and let the boat do the work; the only thing I have to do is fully surrender. I am not at the steering wheel of the boat, nor am I at the steering wheel of life. God has a much bigger and better plan than the one we can see. When you realize that all of your challenges are the greatest blessings, then things become effortless. You surrender. Instead of going upstream, you go downstream, with the current of life, choosing each experience and showing up fully present to experience each moment. The bumps will still be there, but with grace, you learn to jump over them easily and effortlessly, without the resistance that comes from fear.

Waterskiing gives a sense of empowerment—all you have to do is show up and be fully you, and you can fly. Flying across the water with the wind in your hair is like pure joy. A support team coaching you on what to do and letting go of the need to control is what will bring the best results. Simply let go of whatever is holding you back and fly, fly. The magic is in trusting God, trusting life and being the best you that you can be.

When you know yourself beyond the limitations of your own mind, you can be the best *you* that you can be and live a much better life than you ever imagined. *You can live the life God imagined for you.* It is pure, exhilarating freedom to know that you stand on your own two feet and glide effortlessly. When you let the voices of support around you drown out your own inner voice of fear, anything is possible!

Karen Leckie is a speaker, agent of change and breakthrough coach, who specializes in dissolving any "fictitious restrictions" in your mind about what is possible to achieve. She helps the burnt-out and broken down live a life and operate a business full of grace and fulfillment. Her Visionary Ignite and Implement T.R.U.E.™ system merges Karen's commitment to clearing failure patterns and creating upward spirals .

Karen holds bachelor's degrees in both ceramic engineering and education and received her MS in organization development from American University in Washington D.C. She is a certified Mars Venus coach and was a member of Lisa Sasevich's Sassy Mastermind for two years. She is a motivational speaker, giving keynotes and leadership training for conferences.

Karen co-authored The New Superwoman: The Path to more Peace, Playfulness and Prosperity in Business and Life *with Maribel Jimenez, bestselling author and marketing consultant. She is currently co-authoring a book with John Gray, PhD, author of the classic* Men Are from Mars, Women Are from Venus, *the number-one relationship expert in the world and bestselling relationship author of all time. Claim your free teleseries training at www.FreeGiftFromKaren.com and connect with Karen at www.VisionaryBusinessCoaching.com.*

Yoko Chan

Divine Whispers from Behind the Veil

The room was pitch dark, feeling almost like an extension of myself as I sank to my knees. It was as if the darkness was spreading out from my body and then converging back down upon me. As the tears streamed from my eyes, I didn't reach up to wipe them away. I simply knelt there in the darkness, praying to God for answers.

"I have nothing," I said. "I don't know what to do. Please, please show me the way."

What had become of me? I'd had everything—I had been engaged, with the stable home and family life I'd always dreamed of just months away. It had all been in my grasp, but when I discovered something about my fiancé that forced me to leave, I was left with nothing, and I had to return to a new starting point. It was the catalyst that literally brought me to my knees. After a lifetime of being addicted to the struggle, I was utterly spent.

I was my parents' only child, born into a life of wealth and prosperity. Society portrayed us as a perfect family. My parents were beautiful and powerful entrepreneurs who lived a lavish lifestyle. We were adored and envied. But when the door closed behind us, out bled the dysfunction and our home was filled with abuse, violence, addiction, mental illness, infidelity, jealousy and fear.

I had always been a free-spirited little girl, communicating with fairies, angels and many other "invisible" friends. I loved that about me. Unfortunately, my parents did not feel the same way. They took me to a psychologist for being what they saw as strange or weird; I wondered why I wasn't loved just the way I was. "Dear Santa Claus," I wrote one year, "you can take back all of what I have. All I want is a mama and papa to love me."

It was at age fourteen that I lost my grip on the rails and spiraled into self-sabotage. I started acting out to draw attention to myself in an effort to be seen by those I needed love from the most. Drinking, smoking cigarettes and getting into destructive relationships became a part of life, and the prestigious East Coast all-girls boarding school I was attending did nothing to dampen the wild child I had become. With my unlimited American Express® card and elite friends from all over the world, my teens were a blur of parties and booze—anything to continue believing that I was free. I did anything I could to make myself forget the inner pain that I wasn't ready to unlock and deal with…

I am nauseous and dizzy from the alcohol on Mama's breath, and I can feel her hot, moist, smooth and naked skin against mine, her long nails digging into my palm as she uses my hand to touch

---

**After a lifetime of being addicted to
the struggle, I was utterly spent.**

---

herself. Blink. I'm lying motionless in a dark hotel room, the curtains thick and heavy, and there is a giant teddy bear on the windowsill as Papa's face looms large and close over mine. Blink. "Mama, Papa, please let me back in. Please. I'm sorry. I am so sorry…" I cry, shivering in the rain and begging for forgiveness even though I don't know what I did wrong.

Life was confusing. Though my years of self-prescribed "therapy" had blocked much of my past, I still caught the occasional glimpse, as if I was watching it on a movie reel in my head. I didn't understand much of it, feeling as though I was only witnessing these events, as though they were happening to someone else. However, those emotions prevailed, telling me, "You're worthless. You don't deserve good things."

At age twenty-one, I became pregnant. When I felt the baby kick for the first time, I embraced that I was a woman of special and divine gifts. I stepped into my own power and claimed my right to live a fulfilling life. I started studying midwifery and my journey of healing began. It was almost symbolic, because at this point in time and in my development as a midwife, I was sort of "birthing" a new me.

Unfortunately, even though I was healing, growing and moving forward, I still struggled through life and lived in fear, guilt and shame. I saw myself as a victim. Although it was to a lesser extent, my vicious circle of self-sabotage continued. Many times, I sank

---

As my sobs quieted, I started to hear the whispers.

---

into severe depression, became suicidal and would be imprisoned like a criminal in a hospital. Each time, I would get a little help, get back on my feet and return to my life much the same as I was before. *Just when I think I am on my feet, the cycle continues*, I thought. *I am an addict and my vice is the struggle.*

Mama screams, Papa yells, glass shatters. I am running in bare feet, wondering if Mama is dead. Papa is running after me, coming up fast. I'm caught, stabbed and pain tears through my body. Blink. Our car is going too fast, weaving all over the road. I am in the back seat, invisible to my crying and drunk Mama. I pray, "God, I want to be killed in my sleep. Please make me fall asleep. God, please..." Blink.

The echoes of my past overshadowed and diluted any small measure of happiness I was able to claim for myself, as if a self-fulfilling prophecy doomed me to revisit those darkest times and replay them over and over again. I managed to raise four children on my own, graduated college as valedictorian at age thirty-one and had multiple business successes, but I still couldn't break my pattern of self-sabotage. I always ended up struggling, depressed and broke.

The moment I finally hit rock bottom everything changed. My world turned upside down and crumbled, both inside and out. It was all downhill. I did the only thing I felt I could do: I got down on my knees and prayed.

As my sobs quieted I started to hear the whispers. They were almost undetectable at first, but something about them made me

---

"If I am the light," I realized, "then I will never be in the dark."

---

go absolutely silent. It seemed everything around me came to a standstill—time, my surroundings, everything—and as I listened more closely, I started to recognize them. They sounded like the voices I'd spoken to as a child, their tone like that of an old friend I hadn't spoken to in years—happy to see me and wanting to guide me through the darkness and back into the light.

I felt God gently lift me up, holding me close in His arms and filling me with His love, grace and promise. "You are loved, cherished and deserving," the whispers told me. "You are His divine daughter. He created you. You are His light."

After so long spent struggling and fighting against the law of attraction and pulling negativity to me like a magnet, I had no fight left at all. I had felt like this many times before: exhausted, wanting to give up and let myself be gone. But this time, it was different. I suddenly knew that if I were to give in and surrender this time, I wouldn't be consumed. Instead, I would be filled with the light. "If I am the light," I realized, "then I will never be in the dark."

After I surrendered, I remained quiet within. I worked hard to strengthen my relationship with and connection to my Divine Whispers, as I called them, beginning every day with a morning ritual of meditation and concentration. I started each day with an acceptance of the love sent from above, wanting to carry it with me through my day so that I could work and live without the massive stress I had come to think of as normal.

The whispers guided me, and I started to notice the messages and signs from the Divine. *How can I be unworthy and undeserving if I am getting these messages and signs?* Each time there was a seed of doubt or fear, I let myself be quiet and remember, *I am God's divine daughter.* I asked Him to take the fear, doubt, and anxiety away and replace them with His love, grace and promise.

In letting the echoes of my past hold me a prisoner, I had attracted circumstances, crises and chaos that wouldn't allow me to succeed. When I began to listen to the Divine Whispers that had been waiting all along for me to pay attention, I became tuned in to the person I was created to be. I began to accept invitations I would have previously overlooked, going wherever I felt I was called to be and collaborating with the people I felt were sent by the Divine. I suddenly didn't have to push as hard to manifest my hopes and dreams to be as they should be, as they should always have been.

Sometimes, I still hear the echoes. But, rather than becoming louder and louder, they've faded into the background and are no longer haunting me.

"You are more than the sum of your past," say my Divine Whispers. The days of getting sucked into that darkness and disastrous energy are well behind me. I have learned that there is always a blessing to be found in every story that we experience and that we never come out irreparably damaged, even though it may seem that way.

And, what have I learned through all of this? What was the "gift" from the "other side?" It's simply this: I have come to realize that every significant emotional experience carries with it the seed of a deep and profound lesson and, no matter how tough it gets, no matter how damaged we feel we will be as a result of the experience, we are always supported at the highest level. I know that these situations always come to instruct and never obstruct and to trust in the blessing of each "gift of adversity," for therein lies the greatest gifts bestowed upon us.

Dear sisters, listen to your Divine Whispers. If you are the light, you will never be in the dark.

Yoko Chan is an intuitive counselor, a mentor, and a master healer who helps women awaken their divine feminine and connect with their intuition. She travels the world inspiring and empowering women to live the lives they truly deserve. To begin your own extraordinary journey, visit www.28DaysOfGoddessWhispers.com.

Lucille Farrell-Scott, DRS

Like a Gladiator, I Rise

My husband, Geddes, called to chat every day about eleven in the morning. One morning in August, 1988, I answered his call and heard, "I don't want to be married to you anymore." His voice was cold, cold as an icebox.

"What? What do you mean?" I said.

We'd been married for eighteen years and had three teen-age children. *We have a perfect life, a perfect marriage. He must be joking,* I thought.

But he wasn't joking. He said, "I'll talk to you when I get home," and hung up.

Our children and their friends were playing ball in the front yard when Geddes came home about three hours later. Without a word, he began packing his things.

I was frozen. I pleaded, "If you have to go, could you do it in the night when the children are asleep and the neighbors aren't watching?"

When he took his first load to the car, the ballgame broke up. The neighbor children went home and our kids came into the house.

He said not a word to them, but to me he spewed his contempt for black women. "I'm leaving you for a white woman. Black women are no good, you're all a bunch of dogs."

Each word was like a knife, cutting, cutting at my very soul. I had given him so much power over me; his words had so much power to hurt. He went on and on and on. *Is this what he really thinks of me?* I wanted to disappear. I didn't want to exist.

After he left, I put on a white shift dress. I didn't know what to say to the children. I couldn't face the neighbors I'd known for the last ten years. I had to get away.

I got into my car and drove away. I left my home; I left my children sitting wide-eyed in the den. I drove aimlessly for hours, hours of temporary insanity that I still cannot remember fully. His hateful words echoed in my mind like a mantra. I couldn't stop

---

I had given him so much power over me;
his words had so much power to hurt.

---

crying. And then it was dark and the rain was pouring down. It drummed on the roof of the car and washed across the windshield. The wipers couldn't handle the flood. As I struggled to see through the rain and the tears, the thought came to me: *I should melt away into the water.*

I drove to a nearby beach and stopped the car. I sat and bawled. I cried so loudly and the rain came down so hard that I couldn't even hear the sound of the surf. I wanted to merge into all that water. *I'll drive into the ocean. I'll just drive into the ocean and disappear into the water, into the blackness.*

I started the car and accelerated—right into the concrete barrier at the edge of the parking lot. Like a madwoman, I tried for what seemed like an hour to get over that barrier—I had to have the undercarriage repaired later.

Then I bumped that barrier really hard—and I came back to myself. I regained my sanity. I stopped trying to get across the barrier and I analyzed my life. I thought I had the perfect life, the perfect marriage.

But the Lord said, "What are you doing, Lue? Is it worth killing yourself for? Is it worth destroying your life? Listen, he's been cheating all these years. Now he's leaving you for another woman. He's not worth taking your life."

And then I drove home to fight for my life. I left the house feeling like a victim and I came back like a gladiator. I realized that I had given this man my life and he did not value it. And so I had to decide to value my life. I had to make a decision that I was worth something. If I had taken my life, I would have validated all the terrible things he said about black women. I made a decision to value myself; I've never looked back. On that day, I was reborn.

I woke the kids up, sat them down in the den and told them, "Your dad has left and he's not coming back. I'm now the leader of the house." And then I began the process of getting my life back.

I had always meditated, but it was head knowledge, not heart knowledge. Now, I started centering my meditation on something I had to live every day. I had to remember, every day, *he is gone now*. Every day, I had to tell myself, *You have to get up*. Some days I would sink into depression, but I had to fight for my kids. I had a

---

I'll just drive into the ocean and disappear into the water, into the blackness.

---

bitter divorce; I had to fight for the house. I had an everyday battle to regain who I was, to become that person who valued who I was. And through that struggle, I began to live the truth of the saying: "The only person who can destroy you is you."

I started to wear a lot of white, because white had been my color of defeat on that day when I nearly committed suicide. I turned it into a color of power, because I was taking back my life. Nowadays, if it looks as though something is coming against me, I put on white and I'm ready for it.

I was very fortunate to always have a very deeply spiritual environment, though I hadn't been practicing it as I should have. When this trauma occurred, the teachers were in me and kept moving me forward. I had been conscious of meditation, I had been conscious of knowing I am pure spirit, but it was different living it. I knew it, but then I started to live completely and fully in the present.

Everyone has a path, a purpose; when you're not in the now, you're distracted from that purpose. We distract ourselves in all sorts of ways. We distract ourselves through television, through being concerned with other people and their needs, or worrying about the past that you can't do anything about, or fretting over the future that you also cannot control.

All that I ever have, even right now, is right now. Two minutes, two seconds from now, I might not be here, I might be dead. And that's not a morbid thought. We do not think of death as being

---

Everyone has a path, a purpose; when you're not in the now, you're distracted from that purpose.

---

ever-present, but because it is ever-present, it is not morbid. I can't love you unless I love you in the ever-present. I can't help anybody if I am not conscious.

When you start meditating, a lot of answers come to you if you are truly seeking. You can't do meditation in two seconds; it's not microwavable. You have to be committed to the course, be committed to wanting to be ever-present in your life. I am committed to living every second of my life.

I use my near-suicide in coaching. When someone brings me a complaint, "My boss is so horrible," for instance, I tell them about a woman who put on a white dress, abandoned her children and drove off to commit suicide in the rain.

"Where you are right now, do you feel like that woman?" I ask them.

They say, "Oh my gosh, no!"

"Where you are right now, is there anything you are thankful for? You may not like your job, but you just drove up in a nice car. Are you thankful for that?"

They may laugh, "Oh, I never thought about it that way."

I always bring people right to the present, to the moment when they are sitting in front of me. And I ask you to be in the present, right now. What do you have to be grateful for? You're living in your now. Again, what do you have to be grateful for?

Recently, I was driving back from a conference in Maryland. It was night and the rain was like a waterfall. I began to have the same thoughts I'd had that night so long ago. As always, I reminded myself, how unhappy you were back then and how happy you are today, like a different person. And always gratitude, always, always, always.

A staunch advocate for our generations to come, Dr. Lucille Farrell-Scott uplifts young people by introducing them to positive and transformational teachings endorsing their ability to maximize their unlimited potential.

She also advances the message of "Living in Your Now." In South Africa, England, Guyana, Trinidad, Canada and the United States, Dr. Farrell-Scott has shared her message of "Living in Your Now" and has been blessed to see the life-changing effects of her word on the audiences she has touched. Through her books, mentoring, coaching programs and radio and television shows, she has helped thousands of people to live their lives to the fullest as they embrace their "Power of Now."

Dr. Farrell-Scott earned her doctorate in religious studies from Trinity Theological Seminary. She is an active member of several community service organizations including The Links Incorporated and Alpha Kappa Alpha Sorority Incorporated,

Dr. Farrell-Scott is a published author, transformational speaker, and president of Caribbean American Students Educational Foundation, an eighteen-year-old non-profit organization which serves healthy breakfast, lunch and dinner to more than one thousand children every day. Connect with Dr. Farrell-Scott at www.LucilleFarrellScott.com.

Emily Filloramo

Spinning the Bad into Gold

*W*hy me? I thought as I sat in the hospital waiting room, ready to jump to my feet every time a doctor walked by. *Why is this happening now, when we are so young and have so much to lose?*

My husband, Rick, an architect, was just thirty-eight years old and had suffered a massive heart attack. We'd been living the "dream newlywed life," working in jobs we loved, traveling and living in our dream home. I was five months pregnant; my mind raced with terrified thoughts. *Is my unborn son going to have a father? Am I going to be a single parent? Will I end up on the streets?*

I thanked my lucky stars when Rick pulled through and came home after spending five days in the hospital, but those niggling fears of ending up on the streets didn't go away. It was a cold, harsh reality to always be wondering: *Is today the day I become a widow?* My entire world view changed almost overnight, and it put a strain on us—I was dealing with feelings of resentment toward the difficulty of our situation and I didn't want to have any more children "just in case." Everything became "just in case," and I no longer felt financially secure, especially because Rick didn't have much life insurance.

"I always have to have a job," I thought. "I always have to support myself, no matter what."

From an early age, I'd had a keen interest in nutrition—I remember being in high school and sitting at the kitchen table in the mornings, reading cereal boxes, because I wanted to learn more about healthy eating and what went into my food. This yearning for knowledge took me through college and I had graduated with a BS in nutrition from Cornell University.

While I'd always been concerned with healthy eating, I didn't want to pursue dietetics and end up in a hospital or nursing home, preparing menus for sick people—no, I wanted to get out into the world, make connections and deal with professionals in a lucrative industry. I was working retail when I connected with someone who worked at Pfizer; I immediately jumped at the chance and landed my dream pharmaceutical sales job.

By the time of Rick's heart attack, my job was one thing that I could always depend on to give me a solid foundation. I loved everything about it: the selling experience, meeting and connecting with new people and the fact that members of the medical community seemed to enjoy interacting with me and quite often took me under their wings.

Even though my job seemed solid, my husband's health wasn't. During the fifteen years following Rick's heart attack, he was

Everything became "just in case," and I no longer felt financially secure.

constantly in and out of the hospital for his cardiac and digestive issues. In total, he had two angioplasties, a quadruple bypass and another major surgery to control his acid reflux. We must have visited the emergency room at least five or six times a year.

I told him over and over that he could improve his health and well-being through overhauling his nutrition, but he didn't buy the idea that the right foods could heal his heart and digestive issues. He wanted to believe that the next pill was going to "cure" his problems. When Rick finally got "sick and tired of being sick and tired," he hired two separate nutritionists, who essentially told him exactly what I had been telling him for years. The good news is, he listened to them and he is now, for the most part, healed from his heart and digestive issues.

I never felt completely secure about never becoming a widow. You are never "cured" of heart disease; it is managed. I kept wondering why this trauma happened to me at such a young age— my life had been turned upside down, and Rick's condition had created limitations on what we could do as a family. *Why me? Why am I taking care of someone with heart disease at the same time as raising a child? I thought THAT didn't happen until you became a grandparent!*

And then, without warning, my already tenuous sense of security was shattered. In October 2011, after twenty-seven years in pharmaceutical sales with Pfizer, I was laid-off—and in the

---

I'd had the rug completely pulled out from under me, cheating me out of a seven-figure pension!

---

months that followed, I became severely depressed. *What now, Emily? No job means no security—what if today turns out to be the day you become a widow? You know the life insurance won't be enough,* I thought, moving around and around in a cycle that I couldn't shake myself out of. What I had known was very secure income and I'd been close to full retirement since I'd started so young. I'd had the rug completely pulled out from under me, cheating me out of a seven-figure pension!

A close friend said to me when I got laid off, "Why don't you launch your own nutrition coaching business? That's what you're really passionate about." My knee-jerk reaction was to laugh off the idea. Start my own business? With what money? With what security if it all fell apart? No, I felt too much urgency about my situation—I had to get another job that paid well; I just had to.

I'd made myself a home in the pharmaceutical industry—it was all I had known for twenty-seven years. So I applied for jobs similar to the one I'd held with Pfizer, but it seemed that as soon as prospective employers figured out how old I was, even though I could do the job, they didn't really want much to do with a fifty-year-old woman who may not be around too long. All the while, my friend's words about starting a business stayed with me and the more I thought about them, the more they started to sound like a calling.

After four months of searching for a new job, I got an interview for a position I really wanted, yet I still went into it thinking: *If I*

---

*I had spent a long, long time feeling
like the ground beneath me was
unsteady, and enough was enough.*

---

don't get this, it's not supposed to happen. Then, it's meant to be that I launch a business instead. So when I didn't get the job, I wasn't totally devastated—it just told me the direction I needed to go.

I could have stayed bitter and depressed; maybe at some point I could have landed another boring corporate job that would condemn me to an unfulfilling career and never allow me to express all of me, but instead I decided to just pay attention to the signs and took the risk to launch—I had spent a long, long time feeling like the ground beneath me was unsteady, and enough was enough.

Because I took matters into my own hands, failure was not an option. In March 2012, I jumped in with both feet to learn everything I could about being an entrepreneur, spending massive amounts of money on mentors and making connections with people who were very happy to advise me. Finally, in July 2012, I launched Executive Image Nutrition LLC, a consulting business aimed at tailoring a personalized, sustainable slimming and health-promoting plan suitable for each client.

While business was good, I knew it wasn't as great as it could be, but I couldn't figure out how to articulate my uniqueness in the sea of health and wellness coaches. In February 2013, when I read a business blog post that said, "your deepest wound is your truest niche" and "your mess is your message," the light bulb went off.

The answer to my life's purpose had been right under my nose for twenty years! I was meant to experience my husband's heart attack and the subsequent complications; I was meant to be in pharmaceuticals; I was meant to have a two-year period of deep, dark depression; and above all else, I was meant to have a passion for nutrition. All of these things gave me a unique edge and perspective on how to help and relate to people going through the same experiences.

Everything made sense now, because all the dots had been connected. The "lightning rod" of my life purpose had struck. It was no longer, "Why me?" Instead, it was, "Why not me?" While you can't change the cards you were dealt, you can win with the cards you have by reframing your story and making the gold out of the situation. I had to take everything I knew, coupled with everything I wish I never knew and spin them into gold to create something that only I could offer—and I did.

Now, I serve two niches—my husband's and my own. The former allows me to help cardiac patients heal and recognize their heart disease as an opportunity to wake up and improve all aspects of their lives, while the latter allows me to encourage midlife women, particularly those finding themselves in a similar situation to mine, to jump off the ledge—as I have—and reinvent themselves from the inside out through the foundation of health, so that they will have no regrets when they leave this world.

No one has to leave their dreams tucked away in a sock drawer, waiting for the day when they are "happier, thinner, richer and prettier." No one has to waste away the years asking, "Why me?" when they could be asking, "Why not me?" Look back at your life, at all the moments you asked, "Why me?" What about those situations could you spin into the gold that will bring your life's purpose into congruence with your identity? What could you achieve if you just asked yourself, "Why not me?"

Emily Filloramo is a nutrition, lifestyle and image expert. She is a "Recover from Heart Disease" mentor and an "Ageless Beauty and Health" midlife reinvention mentor. Begin your journey to being alive, healthy and beautifully radiant for your life's defining moments at www. AgelessBeautyAndHealth.com and www.RecoverFromHeartDisease. com.

Denise Antoon, JD

On My Own Terms

The honking horns and countless conversations of Manhattan played a dramatic background soundtrack as our limo pulled up to the studio. Three moms from California were about to be guests on *Fox and Friends*. I tried not to gawk at the familiar faces of TV personalities as technicians applied our makeup.

"Wasn't it exciting to meet Al Roker at his office?" whispered the mom next to me. I smiled at her. It *was* exciting. Although I had long since given up my childhood fantasies of stardom in favor of the business side of Hollywood, it seemed fate had intervened. We had been asked to star in a Lifetime reality show. The show would be about our work as private investigators, not silly, but positive—about empowered women doing powerful work while successfully raising families. We all knew that this New York publicity tour was just the start of bigger and better things.

It seemed my life had come full circle. As a young girl, I was fascinated by Hollywood and dreamed of becoming a famous actress. When I went to college, I majored in theater and drama, though I changed my major when I decided to attend law school. Somehow I was inexorably drawn to the business aspects of the entertainment industry. I met many famous stars in my work with a talent agency and a small film production company, handling public relations within the art and music fields and then business and legal affairs at a major network studio as well as talent management.

I was working with several big names in the industry and getting some great experience in film, TV and music. After four years of juggling work, extensive travel and raising children, I looked for work in line with my intellectual interests and passions that would still allow me to be with my children.

For me, success does not mean earning a lot of money so much as achieving balance between work and home. I found an ad online seeking undercover investigators (PIs), work that offered flexible hours with the potential for national media coverage. *Now this is intriguing,* I thought. At the interview a really intelligent, strong woman told me, "The job involves investigative work, developing an online and live training program as well as possible media appearances." The opportunity seemed to perfect for me.

For the next two years, I worked on a lot of cases—some undercover, and some really boring paper-pushing cases. I was part of an awesome team of women (almost all moms) and one

---

We all knew that this New York publicity tour was just the start of bigger and better things.

---

man (the boss). He was actively seeking media exposure for the "PI Moms." *People* magazine ran a story and, once that hit newsstands, the phone was ringing off the hook with requests from media, producers and networks who wanted to work with the moms.

We were given the star treatment, appearing on *The TODAY Show* and in an hour-long episode on *Dr. Phil* devoted to our cool job. We appeared on many radio and local television shows, and were flown to New York City to appear on *Fox and Friends*. When the prospect of a reality show came up, we signed with the Lifetime network because it focused on empowering women. Lifetime signed us for eight episodes to start. We all saw a great opportunity to pay for college for our kids and more. And as for me, I would be in front of the camera at last.

The three months of shooting were a dream come true. Crew members and PI moms became like one big family. The cameras followed us on cases and at home to show how we successfully juggled work and family responsibilities. We celebrated birthdays together; we shared deeply personal information.

And then things went horribly awry. We would go out to film evidence that someone was cheating on workers' compensation, for example, and the subject we were investigating wouldn't be there. "We can't use this," the producers would say. "If we can't get film, we'll have to pull the plug." And they did. Fifty or sixty crew and cast members wept together when the producers announced that the show was over. But the trouble was just beginning.

Two days later, our boss was arrested. He had been working with some current and former police officers selling drugs, running a

---

And then things went horribly awry.

---

brothel and engaging in other crimes. That was in February, 2011, and as the investigation widened, people continued to be arrested into 2013. We learned that one of our boss's staff had been working undercover for the government—and that person had been tipping off our subjects and ruining both our investigations and Lifetime's filming opportunities.

When the District Attorney and federal agents came to speak with me, I worried. *Do I need an attorney? I did nothing wrong. Why would I need a lawyer? But so many people in positions of power are involved. Whom can I trust? Will we moms be wrongfully arrested? Innocent people do get arrested.* I was terrified, but I told the truth.

Within twenty-four hours of our boss's arrest, the media was presenting one negative story after another—about the moms, rather than the corrupt cops. We hadn't had an inkling of what our boss was doing, and suddenly we were labeled drug dealers and prostitutes. Corrupt cops are boring, but moms in suburbia doing these things make a story. People who didn't know us used blogs and social media to say how horrible we were. I felt helpless. My dream was ripped away from me, my reputation tarnished with lies and assumptions.

Some stories didn't even focus on the boss, concentrating more on us moms and our kids. We all wanted to set the record straight, but when one mom tried, they just ripped her apart and made her look even worse. So we all made a pact not to say anything to the media. Still, the media hounded us. One reporter even said, "If you were good mothers, you would speak to the press."

Seeing my face on TV with all those lies made me so incredibly sad and angry. We were a long way from the exciting days of our New York press tour. The dream had become a nightmare. Sleepless

---

**The people who are important
to you know the truth.**

---

nights, my stomach tied up in knots—it was an awful, awful time. I worried constantly. *Will I lose my jobs teaching online courses in criminal justice? What if my students see this?* It was the final straw for my marriage; my husband and I now live in different states.

It took another six months before I could think, *Okay, I'm going to forget all this; I can overcome it and move forward.* I'd have a good day, *I'm not thinking about it*, and then I'd get a text, "Do you know that *20/20* is going to air something?" or "So-and-so wrote an article about it" or "You're on this blog." And I'd cry and then I'd get mad. And as soon as I got over that, another piece would come out.

Things changed when I decided to stand up and take my life back by starting my own business. *I won't let the media or those men destroy my dreams, or the life I want for my family. My experiences in the entertainment industry were great for the most part, so why let this one instance destroy my passion?* I decided to focus on public relations and events, helping people become celebrities in their own fields. My objective had been to empower women. This time, I would make it happen on my own terms.

Today I see my ordeal as a learning experience, a trial by fire I use to help my clients. Publicity has positive and negative aspects. I tell my clients, "You may experience the negative, whether it's small-town gossip or you're out there on TV and people across the nation are gossiping about you. The key is to prepare for it." The greater your celebrity status, the more people seem to love focusing on the negative—like building an idol just to tear it down. The anonymity of social media lets strangers assassinate your character.

Prepare for both the positive and the negative. Let your family and friends know what you're doing and practice fielding questions with them. Keep in mind that you will not be the editor when you appear on *The TODAY Show*, and that what you say might be misconstrued. And if you are attacked, you know yourself; you know the truth. The people who are important to you know the truth. Your family and friends know who you are. Hold onto that and move forward. The journey may not be a straight road, but if you keep moving, eventually you will meet—and possibly exceed—your goals.

I urge my clients to be patient—no one is really an overnight success. When a client gets the coverage that was their goal—that's exciting for me. And if it happened during a week when I also watched my child's soccer game, I feel truly successful.

Denise Antoon, MS, JD, founded the Antoon Group. She leverages her experience in the entertainment industry and her extensive knowledge of media to help people become celebrities in their own industries. Like many young girls, she dreamed of making it big in Hollywood and began college as a theater major. She quickly discovered she loved the business of Hollywood. Denise held professional positions in talent acquisition through a well-known talent agency, in casting at a small film-production company, in public relations within the art and music fields, in business and legal affairs at a major network studio and in talent management—all with many of Hollywood's big names. She has extensive experience budgeting, scheduling, coordinating and supervising large and small media events.

Denise attended law school to further her career and worked as a jury consultant on several celebrity criminal cases. She has appeared on The TODAY Show, Fox and Friends, Dr. Phil *and several local news programs; been interviewed on national radio shows; and featured in* People *magazine. Denise teaches at several universities at both the undergraduate and graduate levels. Through the Antoon Group, she coaches clients one-on-one and created The Celebrity Equation™, a step-by-step program to help anyone reach celebrity status within their field through media and events. Connect with Denise at www. AntoonGroup.com.*

Rebecca Hall Gruyter

Beautifully and Wonderfully Made

I am sitting on a stage in front of a hundred and fifty people, getting ready to stand up and give a presentation. I have my notes at hand, and I know exactly what to say. I feel ready.

When my turn comes, I am introduced to the audience and they politely applaud. As I stand up and approach the podium, I breathe slowly and deeply, prepared to share my full story for the first time. Lights are trained on me and silence falls over the crowd. They are expecting a traditional testimonial… yet I know that there is at least one person in the audience who needs to hear my story, that this message is for them…

There was a time when the thought of speaking in front of a classroom of students, saying my name and answering a simple question—let alone giving a motivational speech to a hundred and fifty people—would have reduced me to a knock-kneed, purple-faced, shaking wreck, but not anymore. *They want you to succeed,* I remind myself. *They want you to have fun up here. They're on your side; they want to hear you.*

Unfortunately, I haven't always believed that about myself. Between the ages of six and twelve, I lived in a home where I was abused and hurt by those who should have protected and provided for me. My life was full of fear, pain, neglect, sadness and loneliness. Sometimes I cried out for help to my teachers, but no one ever really believed me; the matter would be brought up at parent-teacher conferences, but when I spoke up about feeling scared, uncomfortable and unsafe at home, it was laughed off and dismissed as preteen complaining, viewed as far less serious than it was.

Life only got worse for me when I tried to seek a way out. I would be mocked and made fun of, have food taken away and be trapped in my room. I believed that I wasn't loved or valued; that it was my fault and that I was a waste of space, time and energy.

***Life only got worse for me when
I tried to seek a way out.***

I felt alone, frightened, hopeless and sad—so many nights I cried myself to sleep, contemplating putting an end to it all but never being quite desperate or brave enough to actually go through with it. In those dark times, I cried out to God and felt Him hold me close and rock me to sleep. I knew He saw the truth, and He always helped me make it through another day.

When the truth finally came out, I was in sixth grade. My classmates and I were watching a movie that dealt with "good touch, bad touch." As soon as the movie began delving into darker issues, it was as if a floodgate opened in my mind. I had managed to compartmentalize and block out so much of what had happened—and continued to happen—to me that it all came flashing back at once. Suddenly I understood why I never felt safe.

That night, I slept at a girlfriend's house. My friends' houses were usually a haven for me, places where I felt safe and protected, but I was on edge all afternoon and evening.

"Are you okay?" my friend asked after we had flicked off the lights to settle down and go to sleep.

It was the simplest question. Before I knew it, all the words I had been holding back for so long came out in a whispered torrent. When I finished, she was silent for a few moments that felt like hours.

"You have to tell someone," she finally said.

The next day, my friend accompanied me to see my fifth grade teacher. She was one of the few people I trusted and felt safe with and as my friend held my hand, I told her everything. Immediately, I felt as though a weight had been lifted. I had shared the truth and I was finally heard and understood!

I was rescued and moved in with my birth father and stepmother—the mother of my heart—where I was loved and nourished. I started to find my voice and learn that I was lovable and valued, that all that had happened to me wasn't my fault. I started to learn that I was safe and that it was okay to be seen and heard. As I continued to heal, I began to look up and around me. I discovered that there were others walking around still believing the lies, believing that it was their fault, that they were unlovable and a waste of space.

It started a fire in my belly. I wanted to help them see the truth: that they were beautifully and wonderfully made. Toward the end of high school, I attended a Women of Faith Conference in Sacramento. I saw powerful, dynamic and joyful women take the stage. As they shared their stories, wisdom, truth and messages, I was powerfully moved at a heart and soul level. I watched those around me laugh and cry, heal and become empowered.

My heart quickened as I realized that this was the way I could help make a difference, share truth and empower and heal others! This was it!

When I arrived home, I shared my realization with my mom: "I know what I want to be when I grow up! I want to be a motivational speaker!" I told her.

She put her arm around me and said, "That's wonderful! But you do know that in order to be a motivational speaker, you have to stand up in front of people and speak, right?"

Not having made the connection that I would have to stand out in front and speak, I was crushed. I could never do that—it was impossible!

When I had to stand up in front of others, I completely shut down. It was like a conditioned response after so many years when it was unsafe for my voice to be heard and my body to be seen; my body reacted on a cellular level. It was still trying to protect me. Whenever a teacher asked a question to which I knew the answer, I would raise my hand. But when I stood up, my body would react

When I had to stand up in front of others, I completely shut down.

violently. The shaking began in my hands and traveled throughout my entire body. My face turned purple. I froze. I would finally give up and just sit down and spend the rest of the class recovering. Sirens and alarm bells rang inside my head that I was in danger, that it wasn't safe to be seen or heard in any way.

The teachers tried to be kind, but didn't know what I'd been through or why I was having this extreme reaction; they must have thought I was shy. When I would eventually sit down, the whispers of my peers dying out, the relief was immediate—I was invisible again—and I would concentrate on trying to get my face back to a normal color.

I believed my dream of becoming a motivational speaker, which I hadn't dared to speak of to anyone but my stepmother, was over before it even began. But as time passed, I began to think about what I had been through—what I had survived.

Now, I was in a place where I had the freedom to speak without fear of terrible repercussions. The dream didn't give up on me. God had placed me in a home where I could bloom and grow; He had given me the wings I needed to soar. All I had to do was learn to spread them.

I didn't have to live in fear and stay small—I needed to honor how I was made.

Starting with baby steps, I forced myself to speak more and more. A light was waiting for me to step into it, and I did so with my knees knocking, hands shaking and my face purple. I pushed through it because I had to; I made myself say anything I could. In college I approached tables of strangers who looked friendly, explained to them that I was working on my social skills and asked to join their conversations.

Over time, meeting so many people and making my share of friends made me feel happier and more at one with myself. I was having fun. I began to appreciate that every person I spoke to was beautifully and wonderfully made, on purpose and with purpose, each having different gifts, talents, strengths and weaknesses. In turn, I became less concerned that I was "different" and let the people surrounding me act as mirrors: If they were beautifully and wonderfully made, on purpose and with purpose, then so was I.

Now, as I stand in front of this crowd, everyone looking at me with intrigue and expectation, I take another deep breath. My hands are steady; my knees are strong; and the only color on my face is the light dusting of blush on my cheeks.

I look at my audience and I can feel them here in the story with me.

I look at my audience and I can feel them here in the story with me. I can feel their emotion, their energy, their breath—and I know that my story and my message are specifically for at least one person in this room. I can feel the power in the words I am waiting to speak and I can see the audience rooting for me.

"Mom, do you remember when I told you that I had a dream of becoming a motivational speaker?" I'd asked my stepmother on the phone before the conference.

"Of course I do," she'd said.

I'd looked at my presentation notes, and smiled a little to myself. I felt safe in speaking and being heard; I was finally willing to be *seen*. I told her, "Mom, it's happening now."

Standing onstage, bathed in light, I look at the audience and pick someone to speak to. "My name," I begin, "is Rebecca Hall Gruyter."

Rebecca Hall Gruyter is the founder of Your Purpose Driven Practice, a CCC Master Trainer™, the creator of Your Success Formula™, and the owner of two successful private practices. Rebecca is passionate about helping women through her empowerment programs and events, so that her clients can stand in their light and speak their truth. Rebecca also helps them accelerate their businesses, resulting in more of the right clients, higher income and increased profits. Connect with her at www.YourPurposeDrivenPractice.com.

Dr. Manon Bolliger

Defying the Diagnosis Trap

Each of us is a creature of stories, inhabiting a present made up of stories of the past and stories of the imagined future. Part of what makes us human is this gift of storytelling, this need to contextualize. We each look at life through our own individual lens, faceted with the stories we believe about the world and who we are. But, where do these stories come from? And, what role do we play in them?

Most of us function in our day-to-day lives without questioning the stories we have taken almost into the very cores of our beings. Many of these are stories we began to believe many years ago when we were children. "I do not deserve love." "I'm stupid." "If I don't do it, it won't get done." "I can't do anything right." "I can save her (him)." "I'm healthy and strong." "I'm sick."

Deep within our consciousness, we are who we are—with or without these stories. But, if we are not connected with that consciousness and aware of how our stories are directing our thoughts and behaviors, our stories run our lives—sometimes, with fatal results.

When I was twenty-one, I woke up one day with terrible pain in my right eye. It hurt so much I could barely open it; when I did, I saw two clocks on a doubled nightstand. I went to see the ophthalmologist. "What is happening?" I asked. "Did I cut my eye with my contact lens?"

The doctor patched my eye and referred me to a neurologist. In the state I was in, greatly fearing disease, I did not go. Instead, I waited for the symptoms to go away. And they did go away, on the physical level. Optic neuritis, a common precursor of multiple sclerosis (MS), is often short-lived. I do not recommend "ignoring your symptoms," but for me, it may have been a blessing in disguise.

I did not have the emotional maturity and consciousness to defy my diagnosis at the time. And I did not yet understand that my body was "speaking" to me: of old injuries to my spirit, of old stories about love and worth that I still held too deep and close to see.

While earning my master's degree in law and medicine at McGill University, I became more and more interested in natural medicine. It seemed the perfect place for my talents and philosophy: I believe, firmly, that we all have full agency in our lives, including in our own individual healing. I delighted in my studies and later in my own practice as a naturopathic doctor. I also fell in love with a wonderful man of great depth who seemed, at the time, to fulfill all of my needs in a partner.

I did not have the emotional maturity and consciousness to defy my diagnosis at the time.

But after one year, I began to feel terrible pain and malaise in my marriage. *Where is the love? Why, why won't he show me any affection?* I felt unseen, misunderstood, rejected in all the moments I most needed love and understanding. And, at thirty-three, I actually felt like a shadow of myself. I wrote poems about a rose dying before it had a chance to bloom, a rose withering from neglect.

At about the same time, I began to experience a tingling and numbness in my legs. The sensations grew stronger and came more frequently; I started losing my balance aggravated by the weakness I felt in my legs. It was as if they had simply lost the strength to keep me standing. These troubling symptoms, added to my history with the eye and a tremor and new neurological exam results, all led to my diagnosis with MS.

I am so lucky, was my first thought. *Most people would hear this as a death sentence.* The diagnosis was shocking and troubling, yes. But, my background as a naturopathic physician allowed me a certain distance from sheer terror. I no longer believed in "incurable" disease. Every day I was blessed to help people shift their minds and reboot their bodies in order to heal themselves.

I had the huge advantage of believing that I had a curable condition. I had seen several patients with MS and was aware that the treatment choices were very limited and mostly experimental.

I had the huge advantage of believing that I had a curable condition.

Because I could not pretend I was unaware of the "incurable" prognosis in conventional medicine for my condition, all I could do was defy it, instead of letting it define me. And I knew that, to help myself, I had to go within, listen carefully to my body and deeper consciousness and try to understand: *Where is this coming from? What is this "condition?"*

So, as I would do for any other patient, I drew up a picture of myself, including all the emotional symptoms I was experiencing. As I did this, I realized, in retrospect, that my emotional circumstances had earlier roots. This meant my feelings were amplified when I imbued my new relationship with old meaning, the "same story" of unrequited love and murky boundaries. I saw that I shared some of the characteristics that many of my MS patients had: weak personal boundaries, dysfunctional relationships, a history of emotional abuse, a tendency to put the needs of others before the self, an inordinate need for affection and love and feelings of inadequacy due to perceived inability to cope.

In the light of a refined sense of self-pity, the mirror became unrelenting. After taking close account of all my physiological symptoms as well, the treatment I chose was homeopathy. As I responded to the treatment, the stories that had run my life became clear to me, like watching a movie of my life, with a bit of distance. That clarity created a gap into which flowed consciousness—and healing.

Since homeopathy treats the whole person, including the "state of mind," you cannot divide the physical symptoms from the emotional and psychological state. This process allowed me to "own" my state and yet create the gap by not "identifying" with it—not defining myself by it.

Feeling unloved was part of an old pattern. I had not felt understood or loved for who I was as a child, either. As a teenager, I had finally ceased to believe that my mother loved me at all. I refused to see the love I was given as genuine and was blind to the emotional and developmental consequences of equating love with being understood.

Perhaps then, it was no wonder I had married a man who was unable to express his love in a way that satisfied my yearnings; he fit perfectly into the story I already believed about what I deserved and how love was supposed to be. But then, maybe, whether he expressed his love for me or not, I was unable to perceive or receive it.

Not having clear boundaries when we met, I always believed that his experience was directly related to mine. If he was withdrawn, I would take it as a form of rejection. If he was sad, I'd be sad. And if he was happy, I was certain I had done something to make it so. I was passively enmeshed in my perception of his reality; my nervous system was stuck in reactive mode, and I no longer could trust myself to "stand" independently or separate enough for either of us to have our own experience.

Now I was able to drop the feeling that life was not exactly as it should be. I also felt freed from the self-justifications I was clinging to in my story of unrequited love and was able to stop second guessing myself and him for the situation we found ourselves living in. In the end, my marriage did not last; but I came out of it whole because of the insights I had gained into my own stories and how they had directed my experience. Having made the choice to listen to the deeper meaning of my own experience, I could literally and figuratively stand on my own legs again.

Over the past seventeen years, I have had three recurrences of MS symptoms, each corresponding to a period of perceived stress. Each time my symptoms disappeared in less than a week; all I had to do was remind my being and my system of the story I was revisiting. The predisposition to view the world as I originally did still lives in me, but I no longer see it as a reflection of all of me. It no longer defines me, just as symptoms of MS serve as a reminder of fragility, but do not define how my body needs to act. I have effectively cured myself of MS, a disease commonly believed to be "incurable."

Any kind of healing—physical, spiritual, emotional, mental—is a kind of movement through ascending levels of consciousness. Each upward step increases our perception of what is possible, of the deeper story of who we are beyond the old stories that we have learned to accept as truth. In our culture, getting a diagnosis can sound like a death sentence, and everything you read and choose to believe about a "condition" becomes pivotal to your outcomes and

---

We are what heals when healing takes place.

---

your success. A diagnosis, too, is only a story and no story is ever written in stone. Where there is awareness, flow and movement, there is opportunity for change.

If you don't question the thoughts and beliefs in which you contextualize an experience, you can stick yourself with a label—"sick," "helpless," "unloved," "a failure"—and go down the rabbit hole. But if you look with a deeper awareness, you will be able to acknowledge that really anything can change in an instant. That means your story can change, too. Create the possibility for success, and it can actually take place. That's why people heal! Helping others to cultivate this awareness is at the core of everything I do.

We are what heals when healing takes place. Whatever story is challenging you—whether it's a medical diagnosis or someone telling you that your dreams are too lofty to come true—you can start to release yourself from the story by creating a gap around it. Clarify: Investigate what you attach meaning to. What stories have you taken on? Contextualize: What lenses are you looking through? Are you really present to yourself?

When you have this distance, you'll find that your story isn't so crippling after all. And, with that breathing room, you can start bringing some consciousness to your experience rather than just pure reactivity. In this space, your body can clear old patterns enough to reboot itself and get started in the healing process and so can your mind. Letting go of the stories that don't serve you can actually save your life.

This is the beginning of faith and trust in your own innate capacity to trust and surrender to a greater Universal Wisdom—so what is the next chapter in your story?

For the last two decades, Dr. Manon Bolliger has treated thousands of patients as a naturopathic physician. The recipient of numerous awards, she teaches workshops on CLEAR SENSES™ and Reboot™ Your Body for both practitioners and the public. She is the author of What Patients Don't Say if Doctors Don't Ask—The Mindful Patient-Doctor Relationship *(www.WhatPatientsDontSay.com), host of the* Synergy Dialogues™ in Health *radio show, director of Cornerstone Health Centre and founder of Bowen College, Inc. Dr. Bolliger currently resides and practices in Vancouver, British Columbia, Canada. Connect with her at www.DrManonBolliger.ca.*

Kim Chenier, Esq.

Surviving Myself

Here I go again, I thought. *You're not lovable, and you're not good enough.* It was the same old story I replayed in my head over and over again. The year was 2009 and, during a rough patch in my marriage, I fell back into that space of emptiness that had defined most of my adult life. I felt completely devastated, and no matter what I did, I couldn't shake the feeling.

I had a great job, a comfortable home and a nice car, and yet I felt like the most pathetic, unhappy loser in the world, because none of it made me happy. None of it fulfilled me, or made me feel like I was living instead of simply existing. Even though I had accomplished my goal of becoming an attorney, I felt an urging deep down inside that my life was supposed to have more meaning. I just didn't know what it was.

When I looked for answers as to why I couldn't shake these feelings of worthlessness, I only had one thread to follow, the end of which I had been clutching for more than thirty years. It took me all the way back to when I was eighteen years old, and five months pregnant by my then-boyfriend, Reggie.

I was young and naïve, but being in a relationship and about to start a family, you couldn't tell me anything. In my mind, I was grown—my brain didn't factor in the fact that I was still a child searching for love.

That was part of the reason why, when the first hit came, I didn't just leave. It started with an argument about something trivial but quickly escalated. Before I knew it, he hit me across the face and I was falling down. I had never experienced any type of physical abuse before and I felt as though I was having an-out-of body experience. *This can't be happening to me. I love him, he loves me, we're having a baby together.*

I was screaming for him to stop because I was worried about the baby—how interesting, that I was concerned for the baby but not for myself.

When I look back now, I know that my feelings of not being good enough can be traced back even farther; my father was not a part of my life until I was ten years old and because of that I believed I was not good enough for a man to love. So when I fell in love with Reggie, I held onto him no matter how much it hurt me, emotionally and physically. I didn't want to let him go because I was starved for affection.

My head told me it was wrong to stay, but my heart told me I loved him and didn't want to raise a baby alone. So I stayed. I don't recall how often it happened—it wasn't an every day, week, or even month thing. It was only when he got really angry with me and it happened several more times over the next two years. I never had any broken bones or black eyes and afterward he would always say, "I promise it will never happen again."

Every time he said it, I believed him—or at least wanted to. The shame and disgust with myself for not being able to leave was a daily weight that I carried for many years.

My fear of being alone and my inability to leave contributed to my agreement to be his wife; the most pitiful day of our relationship came just four days after we got married. I was dressed in my beautiful lilac-colored dress, with my hair and makeup done, ready to go to our reception, and I don't recall what was said but we got into an argument and Reg started hitting me.

I remember being on the floor on the side of our bed, screaming, "Please, *please* stop hitting me!" When he was finished, I got up, fixed my hair, freshened up my makeup and together we went to the reception as if nothing had ever happened.

I have pictures of us from that day, smiling as if we were so in love, and no one knew that less than an hour before, I was lying on the floor begging my husband to stop beating the crap out of me.

Six months later, I finally found the courage to end the marriage. Even then, I was leaving him more for my daughter's sake than my own. Although Reg had never laid a hand on her and I didn't believe he ever would, I wanted to get her out of that abusive environment. I was finally free, or so I thought.

I was so ashamed of what happened to me and I had so much guilt over staying in that relationship that I continually beat myself up for it. To any outsider, it would appear that things were good and I was a hard-working single mom, making a good life for my

---

*Before I knew it, he hit me across
the face and I was falling down.*

---

daughter, raising her with lots of love. But when it came to me, I lived a phony existence. I wore a mask that covered up the hurt, pain and scars from my past.

At the age of twenty-three, I was diagnosed with an ulcer and it became a metaphor for how this deep, dark secret from my past was eating me up from the inside out. No one had any idea how much I tormented myself with baseless ideas of worthlessness and being "damaged goods." And even though the physical abuse was over, the emotional abuse continued. I had unknowingly stepped into the role of abuser and was emotionally beating myself up on a daily basis.

It wasn't until Reg was tragically killed in a car accident, ten years after we split, that I was able to forgive him. What I didn't understand at the time was that the person who really needed to be forgiven was me.

Over the years I went through many ups and downs. Reg's death prompted me to do something with my life, and I enrolled in college and graduated from law school seven years later. During this period, I suffered from chronic back pain medically caused by a herniated disk. In reality, I believe my back pain was due to self-imposed stress and fear that someone would find out my secret. This, however, would not be my biggest health challenge.

One day, at the beginning of my third year of law school, I suddenly became dizzy and stumbled into a wall. It happened again about an hour later and this time my ears rang and my vision was fuzzy. I drove myself to the emergency room. Through a battery of

---

*I finally found the courage
to end the marriage.*

---

tests, the doctors discovered a blood clot that had traveled through my body and become lodged behind my right eye.

"People usually die when a clot this size reaches their heart or brain," the doctors told me; they were quite amazed that I was still alive.

Thank goodness, I had an extra set of veins behind my right eye, which were too small for the clot to travel through, so it had become lodged there. Two months later, the doctors were equally amazed that they still could not determine either the reason the clot had formed or how it could then dissolve far more quickly than predicted. Despite some permanent loss of vision in my right eye, I was grateful for my life. Still, something wasn't right. I asked myself, "I've survived abuse and a life-threatening blood clot. Why do I still feel so empty?"

Through those early, scary months and years after leaving Reg, my daughter had become my world. She was my reason for living. I don't know what I would have done without her, because she saved me from myself. I was depressed, but she kept me functioning—I could get out of bed in the morning and face life because of her. When she left for college, I fell apart. All of my adult life I had been a mother; it was my entire identity. And while I had things to keep me occupied, when she left, I had nothing to keep me happy.

I was still living with the notion that it took someone else to make me happy. I was searching, but searching for what? *I have a good life, I've remarried and accomplished so much. Why doesn't my view of myself match up with the person I pretend to be?* I spent too much energy "faking it" and not enough energy healing my broken life. I didn't stop to take care of me until 2009, when I was faced with the possibility of my marriage falling apart. I was finally tired of pretending that I was okay, and exhausted from reliving the broken record of my past: *You're not good enough.* It was time to heal.

Reg was dead and I had forgiven him, but the very deep guilt and shame inside of me still existed. I had to finally get to the root of why I was not able to move on from the abuse of so many years ago. I went all out to find an answer; I read self-help books, saw a therapist, cried on a regular basis and prayed hard and often. Then finally it all came together, and I saw that the answer I had been searching for was there all along: I had not forgiven myself. All my adult life, I'd been holding myself responsible for something that was not my fault and had never been my fault.

In order to forgive myself, I had to understand and see clearly that I was so young and so emotionally needy that I made choices back then that I would not make today. That didn't make me a bad person, it made me human! I had to accept my past for exactly

---

I'd been holding myself responsible for something that was not my fault.

---

what it was: the *past.* I couldn't erase it or continue to pretend it never happened, but I could choose to let it go. I would no longer let it be the soundtrack of my life.

Today, I can say I am truly happy. I used to think I didn't have a voice, but now I know my voice is strong and needs to be heard. I now know my difficult journey was necessary for me to learn one of life's greatest lessons: forgiveness. I also know that my life matters. When I think about my life, I no longer define it by abuse or illness or pain or shame or guilt. I have stopped blaming myself for decisions I made when I was eighteen years old.

I am a survivor of many things, but mostly a survivor of myself. I accept myself for who I am and I start from there. My challenge to you is to ask yourself this question: "What would my life be like if I were free from my past?"

Kim Chenier, Esq., is a life and business coach, and an expert in transforming the life you have into the life you love. She earned her JD at Loyola Law School, Los Angeles. Kim believes that we should all live a life in which our emotional and physical wellbeing is such that we feel like a million dollars, every day. To learn more about creating your million-dollar life, visit www.KimChenier.com.

Bianca Echeveste

Own Your Own Mind

H e sat on a stool at the long coffee counter in the new Basque restaurant. Ramon was a short, stocky, gray-haired man with a loud, commanding voice. He owned the restaurant and when he spoke in his loud voice, everyone listened. I was the new waitress. I tiptoed around him.

The year was 1991, and I was seventeen years old. Because of dysfunction at home, my twenty-one-year-old sister and I were on our own. Neither of us earned much, and paying the rent on our little apartment seemed much more important than finishing high school—I could always go back and graduate. Now, I needed this job. And, scary as he seemed at first, I would learn that I needed Ramon, too.

I wouldn't be a waitress forever; I had big plans. I was modeling, and the event that would be my big break was coming up in December: the "Miss America" pageant for Latinas, Nuestra Belleza. I had bought my dresses, my shoes, my accessories. And then I met Roman, Ramon's son. He was older than I, handsome and charismatic. Unlike those boys who sweet-talked me, trying to get their way, Roman was never effusive. When he paid me a compliment, he simply meant it.

Roman swept me off my feet like a whirlwind. I met him in March and was pregnant in April. Pregnant in April meant no pageant in December. Roman proposed, but I refused, even though my dreams were shattered and I felt so horribly alone. I wanted to be sure he really loved me and didn't just want to do "the right thing." I didn't want a quickie marriage followed shortly by divorce. I told Roman, "I don't want to ever question why you decided to marry me."

We were so very different. He was twenty-one, which seemed a lot older to me. We had different religions. He came from a wealthy family; my three sisters and I had slept on the porch of our one-bedroom house. Growing up, I had never realized just how poor

---

He who owns his own mind owns everything!

---

we were—everyone around me was in the same boat—but now I could see so many differences. Roman was a first-generation American, raised in and imbued with a very different culture. In his community, children lived at home, working and saving until—in their thirties—they could buy a house. Only then would they look for someone to marry.

By December, Roman had convinced me that he really, truly loved me, that he wanted to marry me whether I was pregnant or not. One Sunday he said, "Let's get married tomorrow. The only reason you're not my wife right now is because you choose not to be."

I knew then, *this is the time.* But first we had to tell his parents.

His mother, Cecilia, cried out, "Are you crazy? You started wrong and will finish wrong. You are both too young."

Ramon cut short the list of reasons we shouldn't marry. "Just shut up and leave them alone," he said. And that was that.

"He who owns his own mind owns everything!" Ramon would say, and those were the words he lived by. He had emigrated from the Basque region of Spain when he was twenty with two pennies in his pocket given to him by his mother, the only thing of value she possessed at the time of his departure. At his send-off, her parting words were etched in his mind: "Make something of yourself or don't come back at all." But he had the dream and the desire and he owned his mind.

Starting out as a shepherd, Ramon worked in the harshest of conditions—conditions so harsh that one of his roommates committed suicide. He often longed to be back home with his loved ones, but he knew he had to sacrifice some short-term comfort for long-term success. He stuck it out and eventually started his own sheep company, where you will find him on any given day, from sunup to sundown, even at his current age of eighty-one. He married, had a daughter and a son, and, through hard work and street smarts, became a multi-millionaire.

Ramon is responsible for allowing me to see, through his incredible example, what can happen when someone has a dream and stops at nothing to make it come true.

Ramon remains a grounded and humble man. I can only assume that he has learned everything he knows through observation and trial and error because he has no formal education, couldn't use a computer if his life depended on it and, as far I know, has never

---

They treated me as a daughter and Ramon became the father I'd always longed for.

---

read a book of any kind. His inability to speak English didn't stop him either; it may have slowed him down a bit, but he persisted and achieved what most people only dream about. He became my first and most valued mentor.

Those first years of my marriage remain a blur. Roman and I eventually took over the restaurant. We had four children in five years. With Cecilia helping care for the kids, we somehow managed to juggle all of our responsibilities. And we were so happy together! We learned to do everything as one family unit, where we all work and all benefit together. I had the family I had dreamed about when I sat on the steps of my old bedroom-porch. As my in-laws came to know me, all our differences melted away. They treated me as a daughter and Ramon became the father I'd always longed for.

I had never been around someone like him; I watched and learned. So many people come to America with a dream of success. How had Ramon succeeded when so many fell short? He handed down advice left and right; I listened and learned. His was a mindset that I hadn't been exposed to. "You have to own your own mind or someone else owns you," he'd say. Of course that applies

---

Know what you want and then go after it.

---

to alcohol, drugs or any other addiction. But it also includes all the ways we trap ourselves within our own past, or in other people's beliefs.

I never did find time to finish high school. My education came through self-improvement seminars, personal development, reading ferociously and, first and foremost, Ramon. As I read, or listened to a speaker, I would think, *I already know that because I see Ramon doing it.*

The best teacher I ever had didn't have a single degree, save the one that he earned by living a life of abundance. He has never read about the Law of Attraction; he simply lives it. All successful thinkers think the same thing. It may be phrased differently, but at the basic level it's the same: Put action behind what you want and have that core belief that anything is possible when you set your mind to it. Nothing is impossible when you believe you can do it—as Ramon puts it, "Get your mind right first to achieve what you want."

"Know what you want and then go after it," Ramon would say. "Don't worry too much about formal schooling. I know so many people who went to school, but then they don't do anything. I knew what I wanted and I just did it."

And he's right. So many people strategize and plan and think about what they'll do, but they never do anything. So many people read self-improvement books and attend transformational seminars, but what good does all that knowledge do if they don't put action behind it?

I have put action behind my knowledge. Roman and I ran the restaurant for fifteen years. Then Roman took up farming and now raises organic wheat, barley, cotton and alfalfa on over seventy-five hundred acres. We began investing in real estate when the market was down and now have several single-family rentals and commercial properties. In 2007 I turned my love and passion for travel into a thriving travel business.

I have accepted that no one determines the outcome of my life but me, and that no one has power over me unless I give it freely. As a coach and lifestyle consultant, I teach people how to pursue the lives of their dreams. I tell all my clients what I learned from Ramon, "If you own your own mind, you own everything."

First be clear in your mind about your passion, about what you really want. Then stop dreaming about it—your success will be bigger than you can dream. Stop listening to what others have to say about it—they cannot own your mind. Just do it. You may have to learn from experience and from trial and error, but you will succeed beyond the wildest dreams you could have had.

For Ramon's eightieth birthday, we threw a huge surprise party. We invited people from his past, people he hadn't seen in years. I put together a video, a collage of photos set to music. Then people rose and spoke about what he meant to them, sharing both personal and business anecdotes. When it was my turn, I thanked him for his love and his wisdom and expressed how much he had meant to me as a mentor.

After the party, he said to me, "You really did good." And that was all I needed to hear.

Bianca Echeveste is a coach and lifestyle consultant whose greatest passion is helping others find the winner inside and reach for their dreams. Over the last twenty-one years, her family has grown their business from a sheep production company to include a farming operation of over seventy-five hundred acres that grows organic wheat, barley, cotton and alfalfa. In recent years, they seized the emerging opportunities in the downturned real estate market and are now the proud owners of fifteen residential and three commercial properties. Bianca's travel agency, Echeveste's Great Escape Travel, began as a hobby six years ago and has become a thriving business. She has been married to her best friend for twenty-one years and has four beautiful children, with her first grandchild due in August. Connect with Bianca at www.WinWithBianca.com.

Teawna Pinard

Live Your Legacy

W hat is your legacy in this life? When you are gone, how do you want to be remembered?

If you had asked me those things ten years ago, I would have said, "I don't know." I was still so busy chasing other people's dreams and trying to gain their approval, I hadn't even considered those questions.

I always looked up to my father, wanting to model his success as a brilliant entrepreneur. From a very young age, I envisioned myself on the cover of business magazines: "Entrepreneur of the Year!" I followed in my dad's footsteps by getting a degree in business. When I was twenty-five, I co-partnered with my father to operate a human resources company. Soon, my annual sales were seven figures. The thrill of success was enough at first. But, as the years went by, I felt more and more disconnected from the picture-perfect life I had created. I was living a lie. And I didn't know what to do about it.

When I was about thirteen, someone I cared for asked me, "Teawna, how much do you weigh?"

I stared. "About one-forty. Why?" I'd never thought about it. I was active and athletic, and my body seemed fine.

He said, "You might look better seven or eight pounds lighter."

That was all it took. From that time on, my view of my body twisted into dysmorphia. I started dieting, starving myself and then bingeing in a vicious cycle. This went on for years, through my success in the staffing business, through the early years of my happy marriage and the birth of my first daughter, Savana. The whole time, I kept it a secret.

I was locked in a debilitating internal struggle that left me totally exhausted. And all the while, I worked constantly; I went back to work two days after Savana was born and again after my second daughter, Lexi, came into the world. I didn't believe I could let up the drive to achieve for a moment; anything good I felt about myself came from being so successful as a businesswoman. But I was falling apart.

In public, behind the mask, I was one person; behind closed doors, I was another. I fell into a deep depression. I felt utterly hopeless and miserable. Trying to be perfect was, in every sense of the word, killing me.

I had known for several years that I had to make a dramatic change in my life, but I was paralyzed with fear. *What will happen if I leave the business?* Probably more frightening were the potential consequences of not changing. *I might die.* Yet, every

---

The whole time, I kept it a secret.

---

day, unmotivated and resistant, I dragged myself to my office. *I have a viable business. I should be satisfied with my success. My family is depending on me—I can't disappoint them!* Little did they know I was falling down a slippery slope of despair. I was a master at covering up my feelings; I never let anyone—even my beloved husband—see any of my flaws, weaknesses or pain.

But one day several years ago, that brick wall I had built around me came crumbling down. I lay in fetal position on the couch, crying. I was so depressed. I felt hopeless and unworthy of any sort of happiness. And I felt incredible guilt for feeling hopeless and unworthy. *I have a wonderful husband and a beautiful little girl, a successful business—how could I feel so empty inside?* Tears streamed down my face.

And then my living angel appeared. Pulling up her little white chair beside the couch, my two-year-old little girl rested her tiny hand on my arm and looked into my eyes. Speaking with such certainty, she said, "Mommy, don't worry. I am here and I will make it all better. I will take care of you." *Here is this beautiful, innocent, pure being, who even at age* two *can feel my pain and so desperately wants to take it away.*

This self-loathing, unfulfilled, depressed woman is not the role model I want to be for her. And I don't want to burden her with my unlived dreams. I knew that, statistically, Savana would be a product of my choices and of the environment in which we raised her. I knew I didn't want to raise my daughter as someone who

---

You are here to make a huge impact.

---

wouldn't follow her dreams. And I knew it was up to me to set the precedent. I had to get a handle on my eating disorder and step into the life I was meant to live in order to be a better role model for her. *But what am I meant to do?* I asked myself. For the first time, I saw that I could choose what path to take. *What legacy do I want to leave behind for my children?*

So I quit my financially stable business and embarked on a crusade of self-discovery, diving into self-development and seeking out mentors to help me heal and grow. I needed the support. I knew I couldn't do it on my own. I sought out other women that I trusted and felt could help me through the recovery process. Everyone thought I was crazy because they had no idea what I had been going through. My husband was surprised. He thought it was a little crazy, too—but he told me, "I support you completely. If this is what you need to do, I'm behind you one-hundred percent."

I had a burning desire to change. So I tuned into what I really wanted for the first time in my life: to heal; to spend as much time as possible with my family; to experience balanced health and a fulfilling career that would allow me to pay it forward with kindness, passion, purpose and gratitude every day.

This did not happen overnight. It was a years-long process of discovering who I am at the core of my being, what I'm all about and what I want to represent. Knowing something intellectually and actually putting it into practice are *not* the same thing; I worked very hard to get to the point where I could love myself and became a confident woman. About three years before I started to mentor other women, I finally understood the role I was meant

You want to be remembered for the
impact you have made on this world.

to play helping women to step into the leadership roles they were always meant for and to lead legendary lives.

You are here to make a huge impact. You are a leader. Every woman deserves to be happy. Every woman deserves to have a voice. For so many years, I didn't think I had a voice; I was screaming inside to try to get the truth of myself out into the world, but I couldn't. Many women are in the same situation; they have a burning desire to release their inner voices, but, for whatever reason, they are holding themselves back. But it's so critical for you to believe in yourself. You have to do what it takes for yourself to find your own path, because your voice does matter.

The first step is making the commitment to yourself. You have to allow your priorities to shift, bringing more focus onto you and your self-care. You also have to have a burning desire to change. Without that, you're likely to resist and quit before you actually see results. You also must have true understanding of *why* you need to make this change. So, on the one hand, you have to focus on yourself; but the why also has to be *greater* than yourself. What is your mission?

For me, the "why" began with my daughters, wanting to be a strong female role model for them. I knew that if I settled for mediocrity, if I hated my body, if I betrayed my dreams, if I never had the courage to honor my own greatness, Savana and Lexi would have much less chance to love themselves and find their own true power. I wanted to give them every chance at happiness and fulfillment. And as I healed, my mission became not just about my daughters, but about all women.

At times during those three years I was so frustrated, trying to figure out what I was supposed to be doing. *Why isn't this happening, why can't I get it together faster?* I came to realize that I just had to trust the process and it was no use comparing myself with other people who seemed to have it all together. That always just stopped me dead in my tracks. It will come together. There is no time frame. It's the same when you set goals. There are no unrealistic goals, only unrealistic time frames. Personal growth never ends—you are always evolving. That's what life's about. If you know what you want, put your blinders on to avoid the distraction of comparisons and self-judgment and just go for it.

I feel very grateful for the challenges that I had to go through, because I don't think you can speak from a true place of understanding unless you've been there yourself. I had to go through my eating disorder and depression in order to serve other women. Life experience teaches us each unique lessons, but all these unique lessons are valuable.

Before, I couldn't even help myself. Now, I live in gratitude. I feel very blessed for the life I have. When I gave birth to my third daughter, Zoë, it seemed like a confirmation that I am on the right path. There's a reason I had three girls, these three beautiful beings that I can now be fully present for. I have the opportunity to raise them to become empowered, beautiful women who embrace their own voice and legacy and contribute to the world in a positive way.

The vast majority of us maybe think about what we want our legacy to be at the end of our lives. But that's too late. We shouldn't be thinking about it on our deathbed; we need to figure it out now so we can start living it.

You want to be remembered for the impact you have made on this world, for something greater than your own wants, goals and dreams. When you're working toward living your unique legacy, you'll find that change becomes imperative and less difficult. Challenges and obstacles are easier to handle and you don't have to worry so much anymore, or spend so much time struggling to feel better.

Fifteen years ago, I had no idea who I was or what I wanted. Today, I live my legacy: I've helped change many lives and will continue to help other women really find their callings, their passions, their legacies and become the authentic leaders they were always meant to be. That's how I want to be remembered.

So, what is your legacy? How do you want to be remembered?

Teawna Pinard is "The Women's Authentic Leadership & Business Coach." She helps ambitious, heart-centered women leave behind the roles they've outgrown and step into the leadership roles they were born to play. She is the founder of Women Living Legendary Lives, an online resource for women who want to channel their strengths and passions into doing work that they love and that makes the world a better place. Connect with Teawna at www.TeawnaPinard.com.

Rick Poole

Surviving Cancer Twice

"I'm sorry, Mr. Poole. It's cancer."

At the young age of thirty-nine, being told you have cancer is a frightening experience, and my eyes widened as I stared at the doctor in disbelief. I swallowed convulsively against the panic rising up in my throat like bile, memories of watching my father waste away under the effects of chemotherapy and radiation coming to the forefront of my mind, and my first response was: *I will not do chemo or radiation.*

I had experienced my father dying of lung cancer, and the first thing I thought of was his pain and misery. I had watched him go from a healthy, 225-pound individual to a 90-pound man on oxygen. I had been the one who took him for his treatment every week and I had watched him lose his hair and become whittled away into a shadow of his former self. My father's passing had made me question my diet and lifestyle and make some changes. As I sat opposite my doctor four years later, I couldn't help but think, "why me?"

All I knew was that I couldn't let the confusion, the hopelessness and the despair set in permanently. If I was going to beat cancer—and I *was* going to beat it; there was no other option—then I had to change my mindset, change what I allowed into my thoughts and what I exposed my mind to. I needed to do to my mind what I had started to do to my body, taking them both further and making them as pure as they could be. My body was a doorway and I was its security guard. Why would I let in things that would create trouble and derail what I was trying to do?

I thought of my body in the same way as I thought of the doors to my nightclub, Spunky's, which I'd opened four years earlier, in 1980. We had the kind of popularity that allowed us to be open seven nights a week and operated under the tagline "For the fun of it." Three or four nights of the week we had a line out of the door, and everyone was greeted by our host—I say "host" because he could act more as a greeter than any kind of real security. It was a gathering place for people to come and listen to music, to dance and to have fun.

As the months passed, I concentrated on completely modifying my diet and embracing organic, healthy, vibrant and alive foods. I started juicing, detoxing, rebounding/exercising and taking the right herbs and supplements. I eliminated meat and other unhealthy poisons from my diet and I refused chemo. It was my

Being told you have cancer is a frightening experience.

nutrition that was battling the cancer and, with my move into embracing a consistently upbeat mindset, I drew strength from the club and its positive atmosphere. There were no problems or violence and it was always a great place to be, a place that lent me strength in my fight, a place that gave me joy, happiness, peace and fun.

After surgery to remove the part of my large colon that was affected by the cancer, I was finally given the all clear. It was business as usual at the club and, for a few years, everything stayed as it had been. We were an upscale, classy and sophisticated establishment where all classes of people got dressed up to gather and have fun. Nothing had changed: The club was still the same beacon of hope and pillar of strength it had been to me during the cancer.

During the late 1980s, however, I began to experience a different kind of cancer. Music began to change; aggressive new styles of rap and hip-hop were quickly emerging into the mainstream and I noticed a shift in people's attitudes and behavior and in the way they interacted with one another. Words like "posse" became incorporated into everyday life—not just in conversation, but the way people gathered and conducted themselves. Fights began to break out, five or six against one, and I found myself having to increase security at the door and, later, even inside the club.

Using television, radio, movies, print, video games and the Internet, the gangster hip-hop culture, intentionally or unintentionally, began to destroy the core principles of life: respect, honesty, truth, integrity, caring and pride. This culture conditioned and programmed young people for failure.

During the late 1980s, however, I began
to experience a different kind of cancer.

The attitudes and behavior I witnessed within the club seemed to be in direct correlation with the messages of the music; I saw it as a kind of cultural cancer, taking hold of the community and rapidly multiplying. I tried to address it within the club by not letting the DJs play certain types of music—or only playing instrumental versions—but it seemed to be unstoppable.

In 1990, we became the first nightclub in the state of Ohio to install a metal detector at the door, after I had begun to hear of guns being brought onto the premises. Crime rates were rising; crack cocaine was spreading; NWA was touring; and BET was programming our community and kids around the clock. This type of programming was more devastating than crack cocaine because it controls your mind, your thoughts and, as Deepak Chopra says: "A thought is an impulse of energy and information."

The images and commands were beginning to be internalized by our youth and young adults and safety became our number-one concern—it almost became a kind of secondary marketing tool for us, to show that we were concerned for people's welfare. I watched it all happen with a heavy heart, appalled and disappointed that this was what it had come to, that this was what was coming through the doorway to the club.

Even after taking the steps to combat this cancer and try to keep Spunky's a safe and fun place to be by installing the metal detector and increasing security, it still seemed that I was fighting a malignant, aggressive and terminal disease. As early as 1991, the first seeds of wanting to get out were taking root in my mind, but what else was there? Spunky's had been my lifeline, and above all else, I wanted to preserve it.

The uphill struggle became a downhill slide in October, 1993, when there was a shooting outside the club after closing for the night. At the time, the fights were frequent and numerous—in just a few short years, the culture had shifted and changed so much, and with one gunshot, it all became suddenly and horrifically real. A twenty-two-year-old man was shot in the head, outside the club that had once been known for living up to its tagline of, "For the fun of it."

After that, many, many nights I would sit in the club after closing and ask God, "Please, Lord, give me direction. What do I do? Where do I go?"

What I wanted more than anything was to stop being afraid of my life ending quickly and violently, as had happened to that man outside the club. It became clear to me that the mechanisms in society were too powerful to change and, in 1992, I wrote a position paper: "The Media's Negative Portrayal and Conditioning of the Black Community Must Stop."

This paper was sent to more than 125 community leaders, businesses, and social and political organizations. I also met personally with senators, state representatives, the NAACP, the Urban League, the SCLC, the city commissioner, township trustees and police chiefs, all to no avail. I began to realize that perhaps the community at large was not going to survive the cancer that was holding it hostage as it compounded itself further and further—

but I could. I had survived colon cancer by changing my mindset and lifestyle once before and I could do it again.

The people in power are the persuaders; the people without power simply act on the images and commands that are directed their way. Intelligent and educated people are aware of Pavlov's research and findings on the fundamentals of conditioning. We are like Pavlov's dogs, responding to all the trends and messages that are sent our way. Blacks make up twelve to fifteen percent of the population, earn six percent of the money, but buy thirty-one

---

This culture conditioned and programmed young people for failure.

---

percent of the cosmetics, thirty-eight percent of the cigarettes and thirty-nine percent of the alcohol. This isn't happening by accident. In 2012, in one Chicago school district, 245 students were shot to death. How and why is this happening? Are the guns killing people or is it the psychological programming and conditioning of the minds that is influencing such behavior?

The gangster hip-hop culture has been the most devastating cultural trend designed to destroy a people. The lack of leadership and a consciousness for humanity has been a major cause for the proliferation and success of the industry. Black-owned television and radio stations and Black movie producers, directors and musicians, sold out twenty-million Black men, women and children for greed and self-preservation.

As Harry Palmer, who created The Avatar® Course, says, " Our beliefs cause us to create or attract situations and/or events that we experience as our lives." Everything we hear, see and read is retained in our subconscious mind and combines to determine our beliefs.

What we consciously believe about ourselves is displayed through our behavior; it has been stated that all human problems are behavioral problems—therefore, if we can become conscious and aware of our beliefs and our thoughts, we can reverse the damage done by the media outlets to our children and ourselves and change our behavior. And by changing the behavior of the masses, we change the course of history.

With this in mind, before closing the doors to Spunky's, I opened a doorway to the mind by developing the M.I.N.D.S. program: Motivating Individuals to New Directions of Success. Based on the above principles, its three core components are: how to stop the violence; how to secure financial success; and personal health.

In 1995, at which point the club played host to a total of fourteen security staff, I made the decision to close the doors for good. I'd been blessed with a vision of an environment of my own creation, one that pulled from what I'd learned in my fight against colon cancer, and I'd spent two years working on a business plan to open my own health food store that would not only provide service

---

We must change not only what we are putting into our minds, but also what we are putting into our bodies.

---

to a community sorely in need of it, but that would also serve to educate and demonstrate how to make healthy lifestyle changes to address chronic issues that we suffer today.

We live in an age when the technology needed to communicate messages to the entire world is in place and being used, and we are not aware of what is being done to us as a people, or what we're doing to ourselves.

The mechanisms for change are as available as the tools for destruction and we must become more conscious of what we see, hear and experience on a consistent basis. If we are to create change for the betterment of ourselves, our families and our communities, we must change our behavior.

In order to change our behavior, we must change not only what we are putting into our minds, but also what we are putting into our bodies. It all starts with a thought and, if we can purge the negative and "get the garbage out," we cannot only have healthier lives, but also healthier bodies.

I wanted to steer people into an entirely new environment and toward the belief that, other than spirituality, nothing is more important than their health. I wanted to teach people that when we change the minds and habits of the masses, we can change the course of history—I'd seen it myself, after all. For years I had watched the wrong habits and attitudes walking in and out of the doors of Spunky's and now I had created my own opportunity to help motivate individuals in need of positive changes.

In June of 1995, I opened the doors to Natural Foods Plus and five years later I added the Juice Caboose, both with the mission and purpose of educating and informing people on how to make better lifestyle choices and on how to prevent or break the perpetual cycle of pain and misery known as Syndrome X—obesity, hypertension, high cholesterol, diabetes, heart disease, kidney disease and cancer—from which ninety percent of the population suffers.

We can combat even the deadliest diseases within ourselves—like colon cancer, for instance—with the starting point of a single thought. Today, coming through the doors to my store I see people from all walks of life, but all with the same goal: changing their lifestyles, habits and attitudes in order to make positive adjustments in their lives instead of choosing the path of negativity and aggression. Instead of choosing to continue the same unforgiving cycle, they're choosing to reaffirm their lives and open a brand new door for themselves. I ask you: which door do you want to walk through?

Overcoming cancer is a mission Rick Poole is fighting for—not just physical cancer, but also the cultural and societal cancer that takes root and grows around the world without the right mindset and lifestyle choices. He's done both, and shares his mission and commitment to change the world, one book chapter, keynote and specially developed program at a time. In keeping with his aim, he created both the M.I.N.D.S. (Motivating Individuals to New Directions of Success) program and the 7 Steps to Become Healthy Naturally program.

Known as the "Natural Healer," Rick Poole is an entrepreneur and naturalist/vegetarian of over thirty years. His Dayton, Ohio store, Natural Foods Plus & The Juice Caboose has been in operation for eighteen years. An educator for seven years, he holds a BS in physical education from the University of Wisconsin, and master's and specialist degrees in educational administration from the University of Cincinnati. To receive your FREE life-affirming poster or bumper sticker from the M.I.N.D.S. program, connect with Rick at www. SurvivingCancerTwice.com.

Diane Keefe

Don't Give Yourself Away

Moonlight etched a bright path across the broad Mississippi River and silvered each drop thrown up by the huge paddle wheel of the *Becky Thatcher*. Strains of Dixieland jazz rose above the hum of dozens of animated conversations. My heart danced to the beat. This was my celebration of thanks after earning my master's degree. I had never had any parties to celebrate me; I had always set them up to celebrate others.

Lillian, one of the many friends I had invited to the river cruise, stood beside me, transfixed by the peaceful splendor before us. "I've never done anything like this before," she said. "This is the highlight of my life."

Lillian was eighty-two years old, had lived in St. Louis all her life, and never taken a cruise. I thought of how she had given herself to others year after year after year and was still volunteering with the Red Cross. Eighty-plus years given to others! And now finally, *finally*, one small thing for Lillian.

I thought back on my own life. I had let so much of my life go by without really living it. It was a gentle trap, raising children and settling ten houses as we moved every three to five years, following my husband's rising star as an executive. My husband's work kept him too busy to parent, but my girls needed him, especially when they were teenagers. They were going through the hormonal changes of adolescence while I was in menopause. It was a recipe for disaster.

My younger daughter was especially confrontational with me. My husband wanted to be the girls' friend, not their parent, and would make snide comments behind my back. One day after I refused to take my younger daughter to spend the evening with her friends, she hit me while I was driving. When my husband failed to back me up, I finally asked him, "When did it get to the point where you didn't trust my parenting skills? We've got a really serious problem here, because if you had told *me* that, I wouldn't have questioned you. We're done." It was the last straw; our marriage was finished.

I cried for two weeks. I couldn't seem to stop. I was mourning my twenty-eight years of marriage, years of putting everyone else first, of chauffeuring, of volunteer work, of sacrificing my career, all for my family's sake. I thought, *I never imagined I'd be alone as I grew old. What will become of me? It's too late to start all over!*

My husband wanted the house and I didn't. Initially, the girls stayed in our home with their father. Later, one of my daughters joined me. My first night in my tiny apartment was exhilarating. I felt as though a great weight had lifted from my shoulders. For the

---

*I had let so much of my life go
by without really living it.*

---

first time in many years, I felt free. I ate when I wanted to; I chose the programs I wanted to watch. I stayed up as late as I wanted and even went shopping after midnight! I didn't have to explain anything to anyone.

But I was scared, too. I would have to support myself. I'd had a career in office computer systems before the girls were born, but eighteen years is a long time to be out of touch in that field—much too long.

At age fifty-five, I thought I was unprepared to re-enter the workforce. I held my first job for only six months. My second job was with a managed care insurance company, which replaced me with a social worker. I was humiliated and still grieving my divorce and the loss of my mother, who'd had Alzheimer's disease. Co-managing care for my mother, I had learned firsthand about the challenges families face when caring for their elderly loved ones. I returned to college to get an updated education so I could hold a good job helping other families have a better experience taking care of the parents they loved.

I earned my master's degree in gerontology and worked as a geriatric care manager, which was like caregiving times ten. I loved working with older adults. However, a lot of older people are afraid

---

But it was the same old story. I was giving myself away again.

---

to let go of their money and I found that I was discounting the value of my services so much that I couldn't make enough money for myself. Fortunately, my husband helped, so starvation wasn't an issue. But it was the same old story. I was giving myself away again.

I was so stressed. I just put one foot in front of the other and kept moving. Then fate provided a sabbatical: I fell, broke a wrist, herniated a disc in my back and needed seven stitches in my chin. I could no longer lift wheelchairs and walkers, so I decided to semi-retire. At first I was depressed, but I was also learning to review my life, finding out who I really was and what passions drove me. I began to take each day one at a time and enjoy the beauty of nature, looking at a single flower, biking, hiking and spending time with friends.

When I attended an eWomenNetwork conference, I took advantage of the free coaching. One of the coaches, Vasavi Kumar, asked me, "What would you do even if no one paid you?"

I answered, "I would love to teach family caregivers how to care for aging parents, and also be an advocate for older adults."

"Then that is where you need to focus."

I had always been a person of many talents, but sometimes that means you are too scattered. When Vasavi helped me to focus, the universe started to support me. Everything began to fall into place and an assistant, the perfect working partner, fell into my lap. That focus led to my current business. I had clarified the direction of my purpose and dreams. I love getting up every day, and believe that I am operating from my inner joy and love.

A friend invited me to an orientation for IWatchRadio. When I saw its format, I said, "I can do that. It will provide me with the format that caregivers need."

That is when my *Caring for Parents Together* talk show began. A year later I switched to BlogTalkRadio, giving me experience with

---

I love getting up every day, and believe that I am operating from my inner joy and love.

---

both radio and TV. When I interviewed caregivers on the show, people often expressed that they lost themselves caring for others, placing their loved ones' needs above their own.

Angela asked, "How do I rebuild my concept of who I am, because I've given away so much of myself? I feel utterly depleted."

That question struck home. *I gave myself away as a wife and mother. I gave myself away as a caregiver and community volunteer. I gave myself away as a businesswoman.* As women, we are encouraged to defer to our families. In the end, we may feel robbed.

I reflected on how I had been forced to rebuild myself after the divorce. And I knew that caregivers and entrepreneurs are alike in many ways. We always have something more to do. Becoming slaves to our work, we give ourselves completely, forgetting to care for ourselves. And, just as in caring for a loved one, we have a very good, justifiable reason.

It's hard to argue with someone who's trying to pay the bills that they shouldn't be working so hard, just as it's very hard to argue with a caregiver that they shouldn't be so focused on the person for whom they're caring.

However, just as airline attendants tell us we must take care of our oxygen masks first and then help our children, so we must care for ourselves in order to ensure the continuation of all the things that are important to us.

My advice for Angela was the same advice Vasavi had given me: Give yourself permission to actually plan time for yourself into your schedule. Block out your personal time first rather than doing all the work and then, if any time is left over, taking that for yourself. Instead, put yourself first. Block in the time you want to use for going to the gym, or seeing a movie, or visiting friends, or whatever you want to do, and then plan your work schedule around it.

Years later, on that cruise on the Mississippi, it wasn't regret that filled my heart; it was gratitude. Lillian and I crossed the deck of the *Becky Thatcher* together. I went to the stage and took the microphone. I looked around the room at all the people I wanted to thank. My partner in our geriatric care management business, friends I'd made in years of volunteering, school, work and network marketing—so many people, so many thank-yous.

But most of all I wanted to thank my family. My two loving and lovable daughters were there, and so was my ex-husband.

"Thanks to my former husband and present-day friend, Ray," I said. And I thought, *I would never have accomplished all this if we were still together. I would never have found my best self.* And Ray, bless him, stood and waved. Not only had I taken back my self, I had my family, too.

Diane Keefe is a professional geriatric care manager with a breadth of experience working with older adults. When her mother had Alzheimer's disease, she and her brother, like many families, were unprepared for the challenges ahead. Diane wanted to help other families have a better experience. She pursued a master's in gerontology, opened a practice to help older adults and their family caregivers and received her geriatric care manager certified designation in 2009.

Diane released a book, Blueprint for Care/A Practical Guide to Managing Care for Your Loved One *and a DVD set, "Tips From the Experts," featuring excerpts from interviews with experts in aging. She hosts a weekly talk show on BlogTalkRadio.com, educating family caregivers about issues and resources in the aging community. She also teaches via online webinars and writes blog articles, newsletters and more. Connect with Diane at www.CaringForParentsTogether. com.*

Marcia Donaldson

Close to Home

*T*hat car is not going to stop, I thought. *It's pulling onto the highway. It's going to hit me.* It was nine at night, three years ago in Dallas, Texas and I was just one minute away from home. Fear overwhelmed me.

I remember the horrendous impact as the car pulled out from a strip-mall exit and plowed into me. I remember the clash of metal on metal and then the four successive blows to my head as my car rolled four times across the lanes of traffic. I remember a motorist who stopped to help saying, "You're lucky to be alive. You're lucky nobody else hit your car as it rolled."

And I remember telling the paramedics as we raced to the hospital, "But I'm so close to home. How could this happen when I'm so close to home?"

By a miracle, after lots of poking and prodding and sets of x-rays, the doctors sent me home that night. I had nicks in my hands, but no serious injuries to my body. My car was a total wreck, and I felt bruised and battered.

My flight was already booked for the day after the accident to join the rest of my family for a Christmas vacation at Disney World. Of course, I wasn't well enough to fly. My mom wanted to fly and be with me, but I talked her out of it. I said I wasn't sick enough to be in the hospital; I had friends who would look in on me and I wouldn't be alone. It wouldn't be fair to the grandkids or the rest of the family to spoil their Christmas.

I was grateful that I was alive, but I wondered why I hadn't died. Not only was I alive, I was at home, not in a hospital bed with critical injuries. *A miracle.* And as I thanked God again and again, the thought recurred: *Just another minute and I would have been home. Surely, the accident had some deeper meaning.* I spent that Christmas season, and many months afterward, looking at my life. *I survived, so I am supposed to be on this earth. There is a reason for me to still be here, so I've got work to do, and I need to figure out what that work is, what kind of impact I need to be making on the earth. I'm not just here to take up space; I'm here to do something, to accomplish something, to make a difference. What is it?*

I relived the accident in dreams, waking and sleeping. I had to pass the spot every time I left home, and each time I remembered and relived the accident—the screeching metal, the acrid smell, the feel of broken glass in my mouth, and above all, the fear. *I recognize that feeling. I've been living in fear, making all my decisions based on fear, for my entire life.*

One horrible incident from twenty years ago came back to me again and again. I was going to Bible school, thinking that teaching

---

I was grateful that I was alive, but I wondered why I hadn't died.

---

in the church might be my ministry. I think my pastor took that as a sign that I wanted further exposure. Our church was having a very special conference with overseas speakers; twenty-five hundred to three thousand people were there.

I was taken by surprise when my pastor announced, "Marcia will now come up front and give the visitor welcome." I could repeat in my sleep the couple of sentences people said when they gave the visitor welcome—nothing new, nothing strange. I started, "Welcome, all of you…." *All these thousands of people are looking at me.* And then I stopped. I couldn't get out another word. I was too terrified. I abruptly walked off the stage, *I'm so embarrassed; I'm so ashamed.* Then I had to take my place in the choir, again facing those thousands of people.

I could have done it had I gotten notice that he was going to call me. But, like most extroverts, he didn't realize that you must give an introvert notice before you ask them to do something like that. And I certainly was an introvert.

I grew up in a family of extroverts. Mom and my sisters had lots of friends. They had many impromptu get-togethers at our house. While they were laughing and chatting, I would be over in a corner by myself.

I wanted to be like them, because it seemed they had so many friends; I envied that. So, I believed there was something wrong with me. I wanted to be like them, and no matter how much I

Yet, after five years of teaching, that confidence was shattered.

---

tried, I couldn't be like them because it was my personality to be an introvert.

Then, I found teaching. It wasn't something I planned to pursue as a career, but I started to teach one-on-one and I realized that I really loved it. But I had to get up in front of my classmates to talk. *No hiding in the corner; you have to do this.* Getting in front of a classroom was worse at first, but after I got into it, I really loved it. *This is my purpose; I really can do this; I can do this well.* I taught high school for five years and my self-esteem grew. I also taught in my church's adult education program and Sunday school. *I can stand up in front of a group; I can be heard; I can have friends; I can be considered normal.* Teaching gave me confidence. And I loved it.

Yet, after five years of teaching, that confidence was shattered. The Sunday after that embarrassing incident, I just couldn't do it. I was standing in front of my Sunday school class filled with fear. I stumbled over my words as though I'd never taught before. *I know these girls; I've been teaching them for months. What has happened to my confidence? It's gone, completely gone. If I can't teach in front of a classroom of ten to fifteen girls, how will I go back to a bigger classroom with thirty kids?*

A few months later, I ran away from the problem. I left Jamaica and came to the United States where Mom was. Suddenly, I was a person without confidence or self-esteem, as though I was back to square one. That's how my life was for twenty years. I became an accountant. I'd have opportunities to teach, but I always gave into my fears, and declined all offers. I wouldn't pursue it. I could

---

My confidence derives from me accepting me the way I am.

---

recall that incident and think: *It's going to happen again. I'm going to be frozen and unable to say anything.* I let fear rule my life; I let it affect all the decisions I made.

As I reviewed my life during those months after the accident, I realized I wanted to live life on purpose, so I went back to what I knew. I knew I loved teaching. I knew that was my gift; I was really good at it. Even though it doesn't seem to fit with my introverted personality, I was on fire, most energized, when I was in front of people sharing my knowledge. *What do I know that I can teach?* After all, that's what teaching is: passing on what you know.

I thought about how, five years before the accident, I had left corporate accounting to start my own accounting business. Trying to market a business was really hard because my inclination is to be quiet and hide in the background. I couldn't be pushy and aggressive—it just wasn't my nature. But I could be a good listener; that is just as valuable. I could build real relationships with the people I met. As my network slowly expanded, they provided the support I needed to be a successful business owner.

I've learned so much by trial and error over the years as an entrepreneur. I learned that being an introvert is not a disease without a cure; we introverts can be our own authentic selves, and that's okay. I learned that we introverts can succeed on our own terms. I learned how to use my strengths to rewrite the standard business rules. Those are the lessons I can teach. That's why I am still here—to teach other introverts what I've learned. That's what will take me all the way home to my true purpose.

Today, I know exactly what I am here to do. I'm still introverted; I'm still quiet; I'm still reserved, but I now have the confidence that I can be anything I want to be. I no longer equate that confidence with teaching, or with being an extrovert. I learned in the whole process that I could get confidence from other things. I could be confident in my accomplishments as a business owner, for instance. So my confidence is not related to being a teacher or to being someone other than myself, to being extroverted. My confidence derives from me accepting me the way I am.

I now embrace my purpose, to teach other introverts not to be afraid to be who they really are, to be comfortable in their own skins. I teach other introverts an effective step-by-step system to help them start, market and grow a successful business *as an introvert.*

Don't wait for a terrible situation, a near-death experience, to look at your life. Make a conscious decision to look at where you are, what kind of life you are living. Do you believe you are living out your purpose, that you are doing what you were called to do, what you were created to do? Use a period of evaluation to figure that out, and if the answer is no, look at what you think you should be doing and take the steps that are necessary to get home, to get into that space, that place, where you should be serving.

Don't be afraid to be your authentic self. Let out the confident you and live life on purpose, for only then can you safely get all the way home.

Marcia Donaldson is "The Introvert Business Success Coach and Trainer." She specializes in working with introverts who are small-business owners to capitalize on their strengths, which are the key to growth, success and fulfillment. She focuses on teaching a proven, comprehensive, step-by-step business building system, from startup to six- or seven-figure revenues. Marcia works with clients in private and group coaching sessions to help them implement the seven steps of The Introvert Business Success Blueprint™. She supports her clients in realizing sustainable business results while eliminating time wasters and having more fun! Her vision is to help thousands of business owners use the profits from their businesses to make a difference in the world. Connect with Marcia at www.MarciaDonaldson.com.

Diana Gabriel

A Different Kind
of Courage

Have you ever been so content with your life that you knew, beyond all reasonable doubt, that you were exactly where you needed to be and doing exactly what you needed to do? Have you ever let yourself be quiet and listen, really listen, to that inner voice guiding you in the direction you need to be going?

Imagine that kind of contentment. Imagine being so aligned with what you were put on this earth to do that each good thing is a triumph beyond measure, and each bad thing is just a bump in the road, because you know in your heart that you're still on the right path.

I grew up in a home where everything was pragmatic, in a community where decisions were weighed and made based on research; everyone was expected to be responsible and practical. I never really fit in and felt "different." In my family I was seen as "spirited" and "self-directed," qualities that were not celebrated. I somehow knew and trusted that I was on a different path than those around me. I believed something was guiding me. Although I had neither the words nor the context for what it was, I trusted it and followed. This "something" guided me to my first calling.

Quite by accident—or not—I ended up in nursing school. I lived in Rochester, Minnesota, home of the renowned Mayo Clinic and had always been fascinated by healing. Once in nursing school, for the first time in my life I felt aligned with my purpose. I actually felt passion and enthusiasm for what I was doing and a hunger to learn.

When I graduated, I was eager to visit my great-grandmother Molly to share my accomplishment with her. I felt close to her; she had always been accepting and supportive of me. She had always been a quiet woman who didn't say much, but this time she took my hands, looked me in the eye, and said, "You are a healer, just like me."

To my astonishment, she shared with me that she had been a gifted midwife when she was young. My trust in being guided was solidified—it was a sacred, grounding moment for me. Though I never had a grand plan, I knew that I was on my path.

Throughout my career, incredible opportunities just seemed to emerge. I followed each one, trusting that together, they yielded the path I was meant to follow. I listened intently to my inner voice, and it was that innate sense of rightness inside me that kept me moving forward and reaching for "what's next." In each of my major career paths—nurse, therapist, educator and now coach—I had that sense of contentment in knowing that I was right where I was meant to be. I loved doing what I was doing until I was called

---

Though I never had a grand plan,
I knew that I was on my path.

---

to change my path. Even when it meant having to leave doing what I loved, I trusted where I was being led.

I experienced unrest when I turned away from that guiding light or "inner voice." One of these times of unrest in my life was when I was newly divorced, responsible for two teenage kids, and the monetary responsibilities of life felt heavy. At the time, I was working as a therapist; I listened to others regarding the path that I "needed" to take. I turned to pragmatism and did what I thought I had to do, rather than staying in alignment with my calling. I did as advised and felt the spirit drain out of me. The inner voice became muffled and distant, as if it was on one side of a thick wall and I was on the other.

When a big exam came up, I failed. Up until that point in my adult learning, I had always been an honors student. I was embarrassed, hurt, confused as to why I had failed and, most of all, I didn't know what to do. I felt completely restless and dissatisfied with where I was—I was unhappy, unfulfilled as if I was wearing shoes that didn't quite fit, that were too tight. Trying to do the "right" thing, I had lost the sense of deep resonance and contentment I once knew.

Ultimately, I came to realize that I was doing something that I was "supposed" to do, not something I was "meant" to do. I was following the directive of other people who had told me, "This is what you should be doing." It was hard work and it seemed I was

---

I had let my head direct my compass, and look where I had ended up!

---

just going through the motions. To me, that was a red flag. I was on the wrong path; I had let my head direct my compass, and look where I had ended up!

I realized that we are all very capable at "doing" what we are "supposed" to do, and other people are good at influencing that. Our own rationalizations become reasons during those times, because all the things we "should" be doing seem justifiable, and pertain to something that we feel is a responsibility or obligation that makes practical sense. Somehow, I had lost connection with the part of me that knew to trust in that sixth sense, the part that had always guided me due north in alignment with my calling.

When you listen to the inner voice, what it tells you may not often seem easily justifiable. It takes a different kind of courage to listen and to follow that path, because frequently you don't get the same type of support for decisions you make when what you're saying, "I just think it's the right thing to do," rather than, "Here are the good reasons for it."

When I woke up and started listening again, I felt alive with possibility. Suddenly I wasn't just surviving from day to day—I was actually excited about what my future held, whether next week, next month or even next year. I felt as if I had come through a dark and restless period with a renewed trust in my own inner voice, knowing not to doubt where it guided me. I had a new lease on life. The path I had felt obligated to take had left me feeling stuck, dull and spiritless—now, I was back. It was like coming home.

I seldom disregard my inner voice, but when I do I wonder if these times are a test of faith, to remind me of my true path and calling. I have to tap into that different kind of courage in order to reconnect with the guiding voice that points me in the direction

*We need to be silent and notice
what is right in front of us.*

of alignment, even in the face of expectations and demands being made of me, and the things that "make good sense." I did what I had to do, but I couldn't let it derail me forever.

When I discovered coaching, I was finally given the language for my inner voice, the knowledge to recognize it for exactly what it was. I had never truly known or understood that this inner voice was what was driving me, nor its bigger picture, the way it had always been like a thread throughout my life. It is only through looking back that I have realized how different I truly was growing up. In turn, I have been able to put the pieces together for myself.

I've since come to understand the inner voice as our calling, or purpose. My belief is that we are born with this gift of an innate calling, but most of us are so busy that we forget to pause and listen for that voice trying to show us the way. We're all encouraged to have goals and a plan, but all of that is so cerebral that we neglect to leave room for peace and quiet to listen, and to have a little faith in our innate gifts.

What gives your life meaning and purpose? Where do you find your joy and satisfaction? What fulfills you? When you might be feeling lost or restless, what things make you feel alive? What passions light the spark and fan it into a flame of life and vitality? Pay attention to and observe your dreams, because in them you'll find the nuggets and pieces of your true calling. Discerning our calling can be like putting a puzzle together, revealing one piece at a time. We need to be silent and notice what is right in front of us.

If you have responsibilities and justifiable reasons for what you are currently doing, it may seem challenging to be silent and listen to and follow the inner voice. You can start in small ways. Work on parts of your calling while you attend to your responsibilities. Find small ways to honor the calling—it may not be your vocation right now, but that doesn't mean that it won't be in the future, or that you can't satisfy some of it today by taking small actions. You can begin a process of incrementally growing into it.

My truth is that when I am out of alignment with my calling, things are just harder. When I am in alignment, when I have that deep sense of contentment in knowing that I am doing exactly what I am meant to be doing, when I am meant to be doing it, it's so much easier "not to sweat the small stuff." In the grand scheme of things, I trust that it will all work out.

Have you ever had your own sacred moment of awakening from an unexpected source? Someone who whispered in your ear, telling you that you are a healer, or a creator, or a planner or a dreamer? Did you listen deeply and trust in what you received? If not, perhaps it's time to start.

Diana Gabriel is a professional certified coach and works from a self-developed sustainable leadership coaching model anchored in resilience and adaptability. She is passionate about and focused on four areas of service: strengths-based leadership, building cultures of trust, building resiliency, and foundations of principle-based leadership. She is also a Certified Dream Coach™. Connect with Diana at www.DianaGabriel.com.

Marion Neisen

What Time Won't Heal

It was 9:30 p.m. on March 17, 2011, St. Patrick's Day, when I got the call. Holly, my niece, was crying so much that I could barely understand her, and I had to ask her to slow down—I thought I heard what she said, but I didn't want to believe it.

"It's Ray," she said, when she finally caught her breath. I had an awful feeling in the pit of my stomach. She went on to tell me that Raymond, her thirty-year-old volunteer firefighter and accountant husband, had been killed in a fire along with another firefighter.

I couldn't believe what I was hearing. I was horrified and didn't know what to say. I went to work the next day, but couldn't concentrate or hold it together. All I could do was think of Holly and of what she was going through, of how devastated she must be, of how she never got to say goodbye to her husband as I did my own.

I need to be with her, I thought. *Who is going to help her through everything that has to be done right now?*

I left work that morning to be with her, and on the forty-minute drive to their home, I kept asking, *What is the purpose of this?* Even today, I still don't know what the purpose of Ray's death was supposed to be. All I know is that I had an epiphany. I knew why I went through what I went through with my own husband's death—I went through it so that I could be there to help my niece. There *was* a reason.

I remember arriving at Holly's home, where many members of the extended family and two of Holly's best friends were already gathered, and feeling completely helpless. Nothing you can say in a moment like that will comfort anyone; all you need to do is be present. I learned this from a wise pastor in the wee hours of the morning while sitting with my husband during his last days on this earth. "All your husband needs is for you to be present," he told me. "He needs your presence and your touch."

On November 17, 2007, my husband Dave died from a rare sarcoma cancer, after a long and hard-fought battle. After that, nothing held the same meaning as it had before. The spa and salon business I owned, which had previously given me so much happiness, no longer provided that feeling. I took three months off from work—it was all I could afford with the insurance money left over after paying for the memorial. It was on New Year's Day, 2008, that the loss of Davey went from my head to my heart, and I believe I actually felt what it was like to have a broken heart.

In late February, 2008, I recalled one of many conversations Dave and I had had about what we would each do when—not if—

I believe I actually felt what it was like to have a broken heart.

the other died. His words came to me so clearly. "If I die first, I don't want you wallowing," he had said. "You are young, full of life, and you need to move on and find someone else."

I realized right then that life is too short, and decided that I needed to work through the grief and move on with my life.

A few years later, as I stood in the entryway of Holly's home, I watched her come down the stairs. She has amazing blue eyes framed with long, dark eyelashes, and when she cries—I've never seen such huge tears. At that moment I knew I could help her get through the long process ahead—Holly, her parents and her in-laws were in such shock and disbelief that they didn't need the heavy burden of coordinating arrangements. And, because of my own experience, I believed I could be of help to them.

As soon as I had that realization, I took Holly aside and asked if Ray had insurance. I wondered if the government provided any financial support for families whose loved ones had been killed in the line of duty. Right then, however, I had to ascertain the reality of her financial situation.

I wasn't expecting full-fledged details from Holly, so I said, "Direct me to the files. If it's all right with you, I'll see what I can find."

That same day, I visited Ray's work to see what insurance he had. His colleagues were distraught—Ray was like family to them. They must have thought I was a cold-hearted person, doing this less

---

We shouldn't wait for when the worst happens.

---

than thirty hours after Ray's death, but it was for Holly. The more I could do, the less worry for her. I needed to help her figure out how to deal with the financial aspects of Ray's death, the accompanying paperwork, the grief and how to get through the many tributes there were sure to be.

Something must be in place, some organization or legislation, to help the families of emergency responders who have been killed or injured in the line of duty. Is anything set aside for them? Why should they have to cope with all this additional stress on top of losing their loved one? I knew well the trials of "several things going wrong at once" from the numerous setbacks I faced in the months after my husband's death.

While grappling with the arrangements for Ray's funeral—deciding who was invited and who would deliver the eulogy, ring the fireman's bell, say the fireman's prayer, and so on—I wondered, *Why don't people make time to have the difficult conversations and to ensure the wishes of their loved ones are honored?* We shouldn't wait for when the worst happens.

On behalf of Holly and our grieving families, I worked with various organizers such as the National Fire Service, the Ontario Provincial Police, government officials and the funeral directors to compile and take back to my niece and Ray's parents and sister the decisions that needed to be made. And wow, what a profound experience it was to have to be making so many decisions in such a short time, coupled with the bond we all developed with the firefighters and their community.

When it came time to get down to the details, I was reminded again that if we have those difficult conversations before our loved one dies, the family has one less worry and stress, no matter at what age the death occurs. There were no guidelines to help decide on the type of casket, whether there would be a viewing, if Ray would be buried or cremated, who the pallbearers would be, what music would be played, whether there should be flowers or donations... the list was endless, and it seemed every time we made one decision, three more would present themselves. *A twenty-eight-year-old should not have to be making these decisions on how to plan her husband's funeral.*

At that point we didn't know if there would even be a viewing, because Ray was a two-hour drive away from their home, still being examined. Holly didn't know if she would see him at all to say goodbye. With those huge tears rolling down her cheeks, Holly said, "All I see is Ray, lying there in the fire with mud all around and wood planks from the building on top of him, gasping for his last breath."

In the end, two services were held for Ray: a public one and a private, friends-and-family-only gathering. As our family members were being seated in the arena for the public service, we could hear drums beating from outside as the entourage of cars approached and over five thousand emergency response professionals and people from the community lined the streets to pay tribute to Ray and the other volunteer firefighter who was killed alongside him.

The experience of supporting Holly was almost cathartic, as it led me closer to finding my own true path. I realized God's presence again, as I did before Dave's death and while planning his memorial. God gave me the gift of calm and peace. Through helping Holly, I realized that my calling lies in helping people work, and even grow, through their grief and helping grievers take care of unfinished business to aid them through to recovery. I would also like to start a foundation to help the families of emergency responders killed or injured in the line of duty.

Time neither heals nor moves you through grieving; the work you do begins the healing and moves you forward. Grief is not a linear process with "stages." Grief is the normal and natural reaction to loss that results in conflicting feelings caused by the end of or change in a familiar pattern of behavior. You will never replace the loss you have suffered, only learn to live with that loss. So many myths surround grief and the ways that grievers think they "should" act, but truthfully, there is no right or wrong way to grieve—just your own way.

In my training at The Grief Recovery Institute®, I learned more about what "grief recovery" means. In one chapter, *The Grief Recovery Handbook* states, "Recovery means claiming your circumstances instead of letting your circumstances claim you and your happiness."

I came to realize that I did this after Dave died, and that claiming my circumstances enabled me to move forward—not to

---

*It's never too soon, or too late,
to work through grief.*

---

ever forget Dave, the one I loved, but to find new meaning and move on with my life.

Each time I hear the sound of drums, I return to the day of Ray's public service, and the emotions come flooding back. I can hear the low drone of the car engines drawing closer and I can see the faces of five thousand emergency responders and community members twisted and downcast with their grief. But now I can also remember Ray as he was and the good memories and positive feelings far outweigh the sad.

It's never too soon, or too late, to work through grief. Use a method that will help you work through the many conflicting emotions caused by loss. The death of a loved one is one of the most significant changes a person can go through, and by ensuring the difficult conversations are dealt with before the death, you will have the time and space to begin the important work—you will begin to heal and recover.

Please remember: Time alone won't help you heal. It's "the work" you do within that time that will help you move through the grief.

Marion Neisen is a certified grief recovery specialist who provides one-on-one, group, and online support. She helps people who have experienced various types of loss—the death of a loved one, divorce, the loss of a job—move on from their grief using The Grief Recovery Method®, and helps couples and families have the difficult conversations that will prevent later heartache. To begin your own grief recovery, download The Grief Recovery Method® Guide for Loss, *a free ebook with sixty-one tips on the experience of grief and how to help people through it at www.GriefRecoveryTeam.com.*

Mary Lou Luebbe-Gearhart, AuD

From a Leap of Faith to a Divine Fall

One of the paramedics said, "I recognize your voice. You're the hearing expert, Dr. Mary Lou." Then, he sang my jingle: *Luebbe Hearing Services, you'll hear what you've been missing!* I had composed that in the key of A (for audiology) on my piano one morning over twenty years ago.

I smiled and nodded. I felt so embarrassed, because I had fallen and couldn't get up—just like that lady on the TV commercial. Then I realized there was a benefit to being "known," maybe even "beloved," in my city of one million people. Even though I literally "didn't have a leg to stand on," having broken my left leg and right foot and ankle at the same time, I felt lucky. I felt a lot of pain, but mostly lucky.

In a second, I had lost my independence, my active lifestyle, my mobility. I was to remain "immobilized" at home, away from my office, my employees and my patients, "living," eating and sleeping in a recliner for six months. I depended on my husband, now canonized "Saint" David, and the visiting home health care ladies who attended to my daily needs.

Like Jimmy Stewart's character in *It's a Wonderful Life*, I didn't realize how people felt about me until I hit hard times. As friends, business associates, patients, family members and neighbors sent flowers, home-cooked meals, cards and prayers, I felt such love, appreciation and a spiritual uplifting. I, too, had a chance to see how my life touched others. Was I on course? Were my life's goals the right ones? Did they involve something larger and more important than myself?

For some time my "inner voice" had been whispering about writing an inspirational book. I'd been trying to make the time in my hectic schedule. Thank goodness, my amazing and dedicated staff worked even harder in my absence to maintain my business and keep my patients happy. I realized my business could run without me and I would have the opportunity to heed that inner voice.

Have you ever wished for time to write a book, sleep in, remodel your kitchen, or take a sabbatical? Be careful what you wish for. The Divine, the universe, listens, and has a way of granting your wish. That Divine Someone or something applied the "brakes/breaks" so abruptly that my ninety-mile-an-hour lifestyle decelerated to a complete stop. Then a Divine unseen hand shifted my life into "Park." How suddenly my life had changed! What a Divine fall!

Have you ever noticed that your biggest and best opportunities are so often disguised as chaos, insurmountable odds, impossibilities, disappointments and tragedies? This was the second time I had to overcome a life-altering obstacle. My first life-changing experience occurred when I was finishing my bachelor's degree in business administration and marketing. I was planning my life ahead with my soul mate, David. We had met on a blind

In a second, I had lost my independence, my active lifestyle, my mobility.

date and fallen in love at first sight—just like the lyrics in a song. He flew a fighter jet in the Air Force. I pictured us happily married and adventuring around the world. But all that changed one sunny Sunday in the spring.

I slathered oil on my bikini-clad body. I thought I would get a tan while studying for an important exam scheduled for the next day. My thoughtful parents didn't want to distract me, so they decided to take a Sunday drive in the country and see a long-time patient who was too ill to come to Dad's office. "You'll have a quiet house all to yourself so you can get an "A" on the test tomorrow," Dad said. Little did I know those would be his last words to me.

I watched and waved as Dad backed the car down the driveway. I looked at my father's face and thought, *I'm never going to see him again.* I knit my eyebrows and waved my hand like shooing a fly. *Where did that come from? Dad's only fifty-eight.* I shook off that thought by seeing myself in a long, white wedding gown and how Dad would be smiling as he walked me down the aisle.

I was deep in study under the baking sun when our neighbor walked over. Mom had called to ask him to bring me to the hospital. Dad had suffered a massive stroke. Since they were so far from the hospital, he had lost that "Golden Hour" for emergency medical care. He was in a coma; machines were keeping him breathing.

Little did I know those would be his last words to me.

I put my arms around him and rested my head on his chest. My dreams of a glamorous, travel-filled life faded fast. I remembered him telling me that the sense of hearing was the last to go. I told Dad I would continue the family business and provide for Mom. I would do whatever it took. Then, I watched a tear roll down his right cheek into the bowl of his ear. I knew he had heard my deathbed promise. A few hours later I was taking another test and getting an "A."

He had prepared me all my life for this moment. My father, a pioneer in electronics, established our family business to help returning WWII veterans with noise-induced hearing loss. I flashed back to when I was three years old. Dad would put me on his shoulders and delight me by playing "horsey." One day in his office we "galloped" into one of his exam rooms where a patient was sitting in a chair and sobbing uncontrollably.

I asked, "Why is that big man crying, Daddy?"

Dad answered, "He's a brave soldier who lost his hearing. Now, with hearing aids, he can understand speech again, and that's what JOY looks like." Dad continued, "You'll bring comfort and joy to people too, Honey." My destiny must have been determined, and I was spiritually "dedicated" right then.

I had helped Dad and learned so much about people and treating their hearing losses during every summer since I was twelve. I was the "kid." His patients had watched me grow up. I cared very much about them and their hearing success. Now I was about to take that "leap of faith" and run the family business as I had promised.

If you continually say "yes" to life's
challenges, you will grow and learn
and succeed, because you have to.

After the funeral, I went to the office and sat in Dad's creased leather swivel chair behind the big metal desk. *This chair is too big. How am I going to fill this chair?* Ahead of me I saw years of study to earn my master's degree and doctorate in audiology. Step by step, I did it. I brought my widowed mother into the office to give her life purpose. I redecorated and installed state-of-the-art equipment. And, early one morning, I wrote a jingle for TV and radio ads.

From that leap of faith, believing I could run my father's business and continue his legacy, to my recent Divine fall, which gave me the gift of time to reflect on my life, I hired additional dedicated employees and invested in more amazing technology and innovations. I found my mission: to transform lives and relationships through the healing power of better hearing.

Every tiny accomplishment adds to momentum and a "bring it on" attitude. If you continually say "yes" to life's challenges, you will grow and learn and succeed, because you have to.

May I share a good tip? At the end of the day write down what you wanted to accomplish, but didn't. Create your "to do" list, then prioritize the items. When you organize at night, your subconscious gets programmed. Just put a number in front of each item and complete each item in that order the next day. You'll get a lot more done, because you thought it out and mapped it out the night before. You will be able to accomplish more and delegate more. You'll be more successful and focused and efficient.

Remember, it's the challenges that keep your life interesting and make you stronger, more organized and confident. Don't dwell on what is happening to you. Rather, think about why and how you will emerge a better person if you stay positive and overcome fear, excuses and self-doubt.

Listen. Listen for your destiny. It may come in a premonition or tiny voice that requires a leap of faith. Or, it may be a traumatic, yet Divine, fall that gives you time to assess your life and follow your heart. When you listen, you understand. When you understand, you love. And, when you love, you really live. So, listen and live!

Mary Lou Luebbe-Gearhart, AuD, is recognized as one of America's most experienced and trusted hearing experts. She is a board-certified doctor of audiology, and has been President of Luebbe Hearing Services in Columbus, Ohio since 1973. Her passion for helping people hear what they've been missing has taken her around the world, using state-of-the-art hearing aid technology to transform their lives. She is a charter member of the Women Presidents Organization (WPO) and serves on the Board of Trustees of People-to-People International. Go to www.HearOhio.com to contact Dr. Mary Lou and download your free gift, "A Guide to Your Sound Experience."

Karen Powell

Principles in Practice

Two key principles have guided me in life and in building my successful franchise business. The first is "act as if." I'm sure you've heard of that one, but I've added a few words that make a big difference: "act as if what you have and are is enough." The second principle is "detach with love." I've never seen that one applied to business relationships, only to personal relationships, but it's vitally important to entrepreneurs.

It's fine to say, "act as if," but when you're down in the dumps, it seems like lying to act as though everything is coming up roses. Adding those few words keeps you honest with yourself.

What you *have* might be the expensive designer shoes you wear with a consignment-shop suit to your job interview. It might be the one piece of art that symbolizes what you expect your living space to be like. What you *are* might mean acknowledging that right now you are feeling sad or gloomy or unworthy and then realizing that feelings come and go during the day and soon you'll feel happy or optimistic or brilliant, and then acting that way. Or, act as if what you have and are is enough might be the knowledge you've gained, which isn't all there is to know, but which is enough to let you advise a client.

I had created the life I thought I wanted. I had a husband, a house, a child and a satisfying career as a teacher. But life happens;

things change. My husband had an addictive personality and developed a gambling addiction.

His addiction was hurting both the business he'd started and our marriage. *I have to find help. Maybe Gam-Anon can help me fix him.* At my initial Gam-Anon meeting, the first thing they told me was that I was as sick as he was. I thought, *Whoa, I came here for help. I'm running around writing checks to cover his losses, racking up debts, lying to creditors, and you're telling me I have a problem.* Back then I barely took ten bucks a week for myself for lunch or whatever else I might need. So for someone to say to me that I'm as much a part of the problem as my gambling husband was hard to take.

I went there to learn and listen and to help my husband. But I soon saw: *I need to be here to help me.* I didn't understand that at first. But, gradually I realized they were right. I listened up and realized *the only person I can change is myself. Even though I have the things that I said I wanted, my life is a mess.* I did create it,

---

I had created the life I thought I wanted.

---

though not with that outcome in mind. But, I had to own up to the choices I made. It was easy to blame other things, but at the end of the day—I was the one who did this. I think many people make a choice based on an intention or something they want, then life occurs, some distractions get thrown in the way. It's not necessarily a smooth path.

To keep on track, you must accept whatever it is that you're feeling about whatever might be happening. *I accept that I'm experiencing despair, and I'm okay.* In that state of acceptance, you can act as if what you have is enough, and that allows you to create all the things you really do want. So, it's an inside game.

Everything is an inside-out job. After my divorce, I knew that I needed to change: to be positive instead of complaining; to learn new things, take some classes and seminars; to try new things; to meet new people and expand my horizons. One of the new people

I met became my husband. With his encouragement, I left my teaching position to start my own cosmetics and image-consulting business. There was always more month than money. But I was energized with possibility.

And then I won a free piece of art at a women's networking event where I was exhibiting. That opened up my thought process. *I can offer an additional service to make myself different from the other image consultants.* I signed on with a company that had a training program.

Within six months, I became their number-four person in personal sales—simply because I followed their system. I also had the opportunity to build and train a team of custom decorators. It was fun, exhilarating, challenging and rewarding. I loved helping clients convert space that was okay into something they

---

As long as we're enmeshed, we cannot see a person or a situation clearly.

---

loved. When clients said, "Wow, I absolutely love my room, and I never would have made those choices without you," I felt so good. Offering and helping others to have a career opportunity that could be both financially rewarding and to be in an industry that they enjoyed was—and continues to be—an amazing experience.

When that company went out of business in 1995, my husband said, "You don't need them; start your own." The principle "detach with love" helped me to develop many ongoing mutually beneficial relationships with clients and vendors. Through them, I received many referrals, lots of repeat business and a ton of encouragement. I first learned "detach with love" at Gam-Anon. It means that you cannot change or control anyone else, but you need not be enmeshed in their drama. Their actions are their own and so are the consequences of those actions.

We become enmeshed for many reasons: thinking we know better than the other person; trying to show them a better alternative; attempting to fix them; hoping to win. As long as we're enmeshed, we cannot see a person or a situation clearly. We keep trying to assign blame and we think we're justified in doing so. But once we realize that the only person we can change is ourselves, we can detach with love. We don't slam doors on anyone; we respect them. We still care, but we no longer permit ourselves to be drawn into their drama. We hope they change, but we know that we will be okay whether they change or not.

I learned to detach with love when I was married to a compulsive gambler, but I find it essential in building my franchise business.

I must do what I need to do and not fret over what I cannot change.

We had our first franchisee in 1998. Working with franchisees is nice and wonderful when everything is nice and wonderful. When we experience conflicts with a franchisee, that's when we have to detach with love. Sometimes I have to tell them, "Yes, I love being friends with you and having a close relationship with you, but my commitment to you as one of my franchisees is your success, not your friendship."

Sometimes people get mad, and they blame you. Accept that and realize that you are still okay. Practicing "detach with love" does not mean love is conditional; it's not dependent on what someone is doing, or not doing. In Gam-Anon I learned that I could still have a relationship with my ex-husband. That's true in business, too. When I detach with love in dealings with franchisees, or vendors or other colleagues, it does not mean that I end the relationship. In fact, it's quite the opposite.

It's sometimes very hard to detach with love. I care about each of my franchisees. I want each of them to succeed, for my own sake and for theirs. Sometimes a franchisee has a behavior or a problem that adversely affects our business relationship. It is hard not to jump in and "fix" it for them. Then I must remember that I can only fix myself. I can point out how I am affected by what needs to be changed, but making that change is up to them. I cannot become emotionally attached to the outcome, whatever it is. I must detach with love and then act as if there will be change enough. I must do what I need to do and not fret over what I cannot change.

Suppose you have a disagreement with a vendor or a client. When you lose control, you become enmeshed, you get drawn into the drama. Every discussion polarizes between who's right and who's wrong. You try to present your point, so that someone else understands it, and you convince them. Then, it's all about you, rather than what the two of you hope to accomplish and what's best for that. The emotional side takes over and the wanting to be right. And you are enmeshed.

You say to yourself, "It's got to be done this way." That's not the case; it's never the case. So detach with love. Take a step back. What is right about the other point of view? Where can you compromise?

My two guiding principles work as well in my personal as in my professional life. After all, your professional career is just a vehicle to help you express yourself and get what you want from life. Applying these principles will help you succeed against all odds.

But suppose, just for a moment, that the odds are not all stacked against you. Suppose you detach with love. If you just step back for a moment, maybe some of those obstacles disappear, because you are no longer engaged, enmeshed, emotionally attached to them. Because you don't need to conquer them or fix them or solve them. Does an obstacle exist if you don't need to conquer it? And now, suppose you act as if what you have and are is enough, as if those obstacles cannot affect your outcome.

As long as you remember that everything is an inside job—healing, growth, change, success—you'll get there. Remember these words from the Dr. Seuss book, *Oh, the Places You'll Go!*:

"You have brains in your head. You have feet in your shoes.
You can steer yourself any direction you choose.
You're on your own, and you know what you know.
And you are the guy who'll decide where to go."
© Dr. Seuss, *Oh, the Places You'll Go.* Random House, NY, 1990.

Karen Powell earned her BS in business education from Salem State College in Massachusetts and her master's degree from Central Connecticut State University. CEO and a co-founder of Decor&You®, Inc., she developed the DecorPlan System and the StylePrint™ Design System, the franchise's roadmap to sell, create and manage decorating projects. Through the International Franchise Association (IFA), she holds the certified franchise executive designation. As a leader in a female-dominated industry, Karen is well-qualified for the IFA Women's Franchise Committee, where she recently served two terms on the board and is now a member of the IFA ICFE Board of Governors. She actively supports several national organizations dedicated to advancing women in the business world, including Women Empowered by Business (WEBB) and the eWomenNetwork. Karen is a certified Kolbe specialist and green accredited professional. Connect with Karen at www.DecorAndYou.com.

Diane Aleman

Despair Is a Betrayer

Finally, my time had come and the much-awaited moment in my career was about to happen. I was on cloud nine, happier than I had ever been. I had worked so hard, for so long and much more than anyone else in the company. I had built my career reputation by taking struggling accounts and spinning them into gold. And, finally, my hard work was about to be rewarded.

My largest account was shipping its three-year contract worth millions of dollars, for which I would receive a substantial payout. More importantly, I was about to inherit accounts from a male colleague who was leaving the company. The accounts meant more to me than the commissions, because they were everything I'd been told I could never have.

Even though I had proved my worth over and over by performing beyond anyone's expectation, I had been denied these accounts on the sole basis of my sex. Yes, because I am a woman. The company for which I had sacrificed my personal life and earned millions of dollars made it clear to me that a woman's place was not on top. I looked at this obstacle as just another barrier I needed to break through, so every day I strived to prove them wrong.

And now was the moment the company was about to do something it had never done before: reward a well-deserving woman for her hard work.

In preparation for this advancement, I started to build a team to support the new accounts I would be acquiring by fighting to rehire two good friends who had previously worked for the company and had been let go. Even better, I had just convinced the officers of the company to support a new account that would eventually make the company worth more than they could have ever imagined. I was ready.

The day my life changed, we all shuffled into the boardroom, many of us with hangovers from last night's celebration. My associates winked at me, shook my hand and hugged me as a form of support. I was anxious, but excited; I couldn't wait to hear what the president of the company had to say. He started the meeting with the usual updates on sales, as he did every Monday and Friday. Finally, he shifted his attention to me. He began to acknowledge my efforts, sacrifice and how my hard work had led to this moment.

I was about to overcome the obvious sexism I had been subjected to and fighting against since the beginning. I was the happiest I had been in a long time.

For a second, my mind wandered and I was visualizing how amazing the aftermath of this announcement would be. These

I was the obvious choice, the best choice, the only choice.

accounts that were about to be handed to me were going to change my life. The best part? I deserved it and everyone knew it. I was the obvious choice, the best choice, the only choice.

When I refocused on the president, my woman's intuition picked up on something strange. His language became vague and I couldn't shake the feeling that something was wrong. He was saying the right things, but I knew this man, and this speech was his typical way of "performing" right before he would close a deal. He was congratulating me in front of everyone without being specific about what my advancement was.

Finally, my coworkers left the room and I was left sitting across from a man I had respected and admired throughout my career. For the first time in the company's history, it would break tradition and open up the senior accounts to a woman. There he and I sat in silence as I watched him fiddle with the envelope carrying my offer. That piece of paper had the power to destroy me or validate me. It even had the power to fool my heart into believing I should stay with a company that deep inside I knew I had outgrown.

How did I get to this point in my career? In my heart of hearts, I believed that what was in that envelope defined me. The money didn't ultimately matter nor did the title nor the challenge ahead of me. All that mattered to me was that I got the same opportunity the men got and a chance to prove them wrong.

He slid the envelope across the table; as I reached for it, I wondered, *If it ultimately isn't about the money or title for me, what is it about?* I opened it, but inside, there was no letter. Instead, I found a typewritten story. Set back in the early 1900s, it was about an old "negro man" who, despite losing everything, including his family, still spoke with hope and optimism. The piece concluded:

There is a special glory in holding on. . .Really to achieve is perhaps not so much to win, as to never give over, and who knows but that our fears may be as great liars as some of our hopes? Despair is a betrayer. The longest and darkest night may end in a day joyous and serene—if we hold on.

What does this have to do with me? I thought. *Is he trying to point out that I'm a woman, a minority? Am I the poor "negro man" in the story?* With a confused look upon my face, I pulled out the second piece of paper. The paper had a list of accounts.

The list contained three of my most prized accounts, including the three-year multimillion-dollar contract that was about to cash in. *Interesting.* Below it were the names of the three accounts I stood to inherit: the accounts that had only been held by men. *Not quite what I expected. Two are completely insignificant and only one of them holds the key to my convictions. What does this mean?* And then it clicked. In order to get the one significant account that meant everything to me, I had to give up all the accounts I had built with my own sweat and tears, including the one about to cash in. Wow, this wasn't a promotion after all: This was a test; he was testing me and my convictions.

They fired me the day the commissions were to be paid.

At a loss for words for the first time, I was livid. I started to tremble and my heart fell as the truth set in. *Does he know something I don't? Does he know me better than I know myself?*

For a moment, I considered the option, because it was what I had been fighting for all these years. All these years I worked toward something that they just wouldn't bring themselves to give me. I believed they would; I really did. *Was I blinded by my own convictions? Have I lost sight of my goal? What does it matter at this point?*

I had been broken. As much as I wanted to be man enough for those accounts, the truth was, I was a woman, and I was about to prove it. I could no longer hold my emotions back. A few tears fell as I stood up, pushed my chair out from the table and rejected the offer. I held it together long enough to get to my car before I let myself cry. I felt defeated. *How could things get any worse?* I knew I had lost the battle, but I had no idea it was setting me up for war.

After a few days, I pulled myself together and decided to move forward. I buried myself in my work, focusing my efforts on building the super team I had put into motion before the supposed advancement. It wasn't easy—it became a battle of its own. No one had faith that these two ex-employees were valuable enough to bring back to the company.

So I fought, put my reputation on the line and gave up a part of my salary to bring them back. In my heart, I was fighting for my friends. I knew they needed the work and I needed them, so that I could devise a new path on the way to the top. I wasn't even sure if this was the right plan, but it did provide a much-needed distraction where I could focus my energies on their fight and ignore my own defeat.

After I won that battle, I realized that my plan had backfired. The officers of the company who had fought so hard against rehiring the two employees were suddenly involved in secret meetings and eventually gave secret offers to my two good friends in exchange for the ultimate betrayal. That's right, the friends I rehired sold out to the company. In exchange for betraying me, they received compensation and the accounts I had longed for for years. And I had to train the two of them!

I still have no idea how I got through it. It was one of the hardest things I have ever had to do. When the training was complete, I received a call from the president and was fired with little to no explanation after seven years of dedication. It was over. I didn't get those accounts; I didn't get those commissions. They fired me the day the commissions were to be paid.

You would think this is where I finally broke down, but I didn't. I didn't even cry. I had no time for tears. My determination to succeed spurred me into immediate survivor mode. Three days after I was fired, I contacted an attorney friend who helped me start my own company in a way that used what I'd learned

---

The hours are long, the money is good, but the freedom is priceless.

---

without competing with my former employer. I had a number of accounts that would come with me, so instead of choosing to sue as I probably should have, I chose to reinvent myself and live to fight another day. I went maverick. I walked into the office of each and every client I had, announced my independence and offered them a deal they could not refuse. I worked all of the time; my mind was focused and my work ethic so insane, it would have been impossible to fail.

The structure of my company and its mission was so unique that many colleagues recognized the genius but wondered if it would succeed. All the years I had spent learning the industry from the inside out proved to my advantage. I understood the complicated industry relationships, and I grasped the big picture. Built upon my reputation of integrity, honesty and doing the right thing, I earned the trust of all my previous competitors and clientele. Armed merely with my unshakable vision, I created a company that was client driven, the first of its kind—a game-changer.

I was going to use what I had learned and educate the buyer of the ins and outs in manufacturing. We started in the United States and slowly grew into Asia and Mexico. Deals were made and relationships built to form a company with a forty- to fifty-percent annual growth rate. The hours are long, the money is good, but the freedom is priceless.

Ironically, the excerpt that at one time confused and angered me is now framed on my office wall. I still read it from time to time. I was right: The paper in the envelope did seal my fate forever and I don't regret that it did.

I thought, at first, that the excerpt was about a poor and hopeless man with a naïve sense of optimism and hope. And it was, but it was also about me. I was naïve, hopeful and somewhat in denial of the limitations set upon me. I never gave in to despair. Even after huge losses, I just kept playing the game.

I look back on my journey now and am grateful and proud to be that naïve person. If I had ever let the truth set in for even a moment, I might not be where I am today, on top and without limitations.

There is a special glory in holding on. . .Really to achieve is perhaps not so much to win, as to never give over, and who knows but that our fears may be as great liars as some of our hopes? Despair is a betrayer. The longest and darkest night may end in a day joyous and serene—if we hold on.

Diane Aleman is the founder and CEO of Maverick Telecom Solutions. Passionate about her clients' needs, she provides a multitude of professional services that help contract manufacturers and OEMs around the world minimize cost and time to market. Connect with Diane at www.MavTel.com.

Sangita Patel

What Have You Done with Your Gift?

For almost eighteen years, the emotional and physical pain of the car accident that killed my little brother and left me unable to walk had ruled me, inside and out. The pain in my left foot was so excruciating that I could not stand for more than three minutes at a time, and every several months I had yet another arthroscopic surgery to vacuum out the bone chips that had collected in my left ankle, where I had no cartilage.

Why me? Why? Angry with God, I cried my eyes out. After all of the years of surgeries and painkillers, I was not getting any better. My health was only getting worse and I was putting on weight at an alarming rate. I felt numb from all of the suffering—I could not even feel emotionally attached to my children. I was up to my throat in grief and anxiety. *Please, no more medications. No more surgeries or needles in my body.* I felt like a volcano, ready to blow up. It had gotten so bad that I did not want to live anymore. I did the only thing left to do: I turned to the universe and prayed for a miracle.

I want to live! I know I have a message to give; a gift to share that God has given me. What am I going to do when He asks me, "Did you share my gift?"

In 1989, my husband, our small son and I went to India when my mother-in-law passed away, to put her ashes in the holy river as is traditional for Hindus. My husband came back early to go back to work, but my son and I stayed a little longer so we could bring my younger brother Niraj, who was finishing his exams, back to the United States with us for a visit.

Niraj and I—along with one of my father's employees—were on our way to pick up Niraj's passport at about 7:30 in the morning when a huge truck, an eighteen-wheeler, swerved head-on into our lane from the opposite side of the highway. Our small car was suddenly under the truck, its roof sliced off, exposing us to further damage. My brother had been driving. My father's employee was in the front passenger seat. They both flew out of the car, while I remained stuck, my legs crushed and broken under the seat, my broken bones sticking up out of my skin.

Covered in blood and broken glass, I was rushed to the nearest hospital, where doctors treated me for head injuries and prepared to chop off my legs. My father was making funeral arrangements for his employee and for my brother.

When my father was finally able to see me, he had me shifted to a bigger hospital in the city, where I remained for the next eight months while surgeons tried to put my legs back together. They reconstructed my left foot and ankle and put a rod in my left leg from my foot to knee and twenty screws in my right leg. I could not see my two-year-old son during this time, because the doctors thought it would be traumatic for him to see me scarred and bandaged from waist to toe, hooked up to machines with my shattered legs suspended in the air. I missed him terribly.

My family waited months to tell me about my brother's passing, fearing that the trauma would be too much for my injured brain; it might cause me to go into shock and coma.

When my father took my hand in the hospital room and said gently, "Sangita, I have something to tell you," I knew something was very, very wrong. But as he spoke, telling me how—and when—Niraj had died, I felt totally disoriented, as if I were listening to someone else's story. *What do I feel? How do I feel, when all there is to feel is pain?* I had no one to talk to. This loss, on top of the physical pain and the loss of my former life, was too much. I shut down.

After that, I was again shifted to another hospital, where I started to learn to walk again, haltingly, with a walker and crutches. I felt like a baby, having to learn everything all over again. Once I had the hang of my wheelchair, my family brought me back to the United States. For the next seventeen years, I underwent surgeries every several months—taking screws out, putting new ones in, taking the rod out, putting the new one in.

By 2005, when I finally reached my breaking point and began to pray for a miracle, my emotional and physical health were so bad that I could not stand living in my own body anymore. I wanted to die rather than have another surgery. But I had also recently begun reading self-help books by Dr. Wayne Dyer and others, and I had

*Covered in blood and broken glass, I
was rushed to the nearest hospital.*

an inkling that there might be another way. So, rather than let the volcano threatening to erupt inside me sweep me away, I turned to the universe and prayed: *Help me heal.*

All of a sudden, as if my prayers had been heard, I started getting mail about non-Western healing practices and strategies. At a retreat, I met Qigong Master Lin. His vision is that we are all natural-born healers and that anyone can heal one's own body without taking any medication.

That caught my attention. Qigong is an ancient Chinese healing modality. "Qi" means "energy," and "gong" means working with energy. There are two energies, yin and yang, female and male. When there is imbalance between these two energies, illness, organ dysfunction, stress, even cancer, diabetes and high blood pressure occur. Qigong exercises give positive information and affirmation to one's body again, so one can start finding balance. Since I could not stand, I could not practice yoga—I had tried, but the experience was too physically painful. However, I could do Qigong exercises sitting down or even lying on my bed. As my energy started to balance and increase, I was able to start turning inward.

As I started practicing Qigong, I was also doing a spiritual course with Master Jeddah Mali, who was teaching about self-awareness, expansion and living in the moment. Combining these modalities, my life changed completely. I started to heal inside and out. I had always heard a faint inner voice—like a heaviness in my chest, like someone trying to talk. I began a conversation with

---

Even in my dreams, everything changed.

---

that voice. *What's happening? How am I feeling?* At the same time, I was having dreams in which I saw myself as a little girl, six or seven years old, crying in a dark corner.

Exploring my inner self, I found my inner child, that lonely six-year-old whose parents had sent her away from home to school in a city hours away. I had missed the love from my mom and dad, and from Niraj, so much. At eighteen, I moved away from India to the United States to be with my new husband in the marriage my grandparents had arranged for me. Niraj was eight years younger than me, only ten when I left, and we had just begun to really know each other. We never got to bond the way I had wanted to.

The darkness that surrounded the little Sangita in my dreams was the absence of the love I had always craved and what I had lost in Niraj when the accident took him and my old life with him. I grieved for what that young girl—what I—had lost. I reached out to her. I said, *I love you.* And, then I cried for about three months just from the relief of letting go and practicing Emotional Freedom Technique (EFT). It was then that I finally processed Niraj's passing. *He is gone. There is no going back.*

Liberation. Even in my dreams, everything changed. My internal vibration started to rise, and I started to feel more confident, even excited about my life. *Okay, I'm here for a purpose on this planet. I'm not just here to cook and clean and suffer.*

Physically, I improved significantly as well. The inflammation in my legs decreased and I could stand up for long periods of time. When I could stand for more than half an hour, it was a huge accomplishment! Clarity finally came within: *I have to share this gift with the world, this limitless possibility for healing.* All those years I thought my future held nothing but pain, but now this gift was made clear to me.

My present health, both physical and emotional, is incredible. My perspective is completely different; I look at tough experiences as ways to grow, and more often than not I live in joy. I give workshops in Qigong and meditation in my local area, and I can stand up for three whole hours. I see a personal trainer; go for massage once a week; eat healthy, organic food and take supplements instead of drugs. I took my last Advil® in 2005, the year I had my last surgery. I still have a couple of screws and wires in my left foot and that leg is a little shorter and narrower than my right (I lost a couple of bones). But for seventeen years I did not know what it felt like to put my bare foot down on the ground. Now I can walk and feel the ground, feel the grass, feel Mother Earth.

We do not have to suffer emotionally or physically. Our bodies are a miracle. We can heal, once the focus turns inward. Knowing your body's systems and your inner self, you can start making the shifts in your body that are necessary for healing. That is

---

Miracles can and do occur.

---

how I started. Your healing depends on how open and willing, how committed and responsible, you are. Everything that has happened in your life did not take place in one moment—likewise, healing is a process. It is like a seed; it takes nurturing, loving care and sunshine to grow. How open are you to receiving the healing energy of the universe? The universe is always ready to help us.

Know the truth of who you are: You are God's child. You are loved, and you are safe. If you know who you really are inside, the possibilities for your healing are limitless.

When I felt so overwhelmed and alone with all of my pain, journaling helped me immensely. The act of recollecting and putting it all down on paper helped me understand and finally see my true self. Try meditation. Try journaling. Try Qigong. Connect with and embrace your inner self to awaken your natural healing power. Ten minutes in the morning and in the evening of these kinds of exercises, every day, will help start the shift within your body to gradually bring you into alignment with universal energy. You will be amazed.

Last year, Johira, a client of mine, came to me crying. She was pregnant—and she told me that when she had gone in for a recent checkup, the doctors had found a cyst in her baby's brain. She was devastated. We did some Qigong. I gave her some active exercises, a breathing exercise, a fifteen-minute guided meditation to listen to every day and some affirmations to say to herself and to the baby, such as, "I am in the universe; the universe is in my body; the universe and I are one. All the channels of the baby's brain are open; all the blockages are gone, and the baby is completely healed." When Johira went back to the doctor's office six weeks later, they were all stunned: the cyst was completely gone. The next time I saw Johira, she was glowing, weeping tears of joy. Now she has a baby girl, and they are both doing just fine.

Miracles can and do occur. Imagine and commit to healing for you, and you'll be on your way to a miracle.

Every day when I wake up, my prayer is: *Thank you, God, for making me your humble and loving instrument of healing. Please send me all your healing energy through my heart to others, so I can help them to heal.* I know that when God comes to ask me, "Did you share my gift?" I can answer with a full-hearted YES.

Sangita Patel is the chief value creator of Embrace Your Inner Self. She is a global holistic practitioner, facilitating and teaching the powerful elements of healing. She uses an assortment of tools and practices from Qigong, EFT, the Holistic Breakthrough Method, Integrated Energy Therapy (IET), Seraphim Blueprint and chakra healing. Sangita is affiliated with Spring Forest Qigong, The Institute of HeartMath, the Global Association of Holistic Psychotherapy, The Tapping Solution, the EFT Universe and The Center of Being and she teaches Qigong, chakra healing and EFT at many healing and community centers, psychotherapists' groups, colleges and libraries in her area. Connect with Sangita at www.EmbraceYourInnerSelf.com.

Sharon Addison, RN

Waiting for the Right Time

I was headed out the door, ready for some "me" time in the sun during my lunch hour. Though it had been an easy morning of nursing, I felt resentful that I couldn't just quit and spend my time and energy on the coaching business I had just started.

Though I knew coaching was where my passion lay, I'd been a nurse for fifteen years. I was holding on to my job with its dependable income and not fully trusting and embracing my dream. *When would it finally be the right time to step into my true purpose in life? When would it be the "right time?" And how would I know?*

A colleague asked, "Sharon, can you please help me with this patient?"

"Sure," I said and walked with her into the CAT-scan room. On the cold metal table lay a very slender older woman with no hair. Her thin arms and legs, her ashen face and her hair loss all testified to a long and serious illness. *What did she look like when she had hair?* I wondered. *Even now, ill as she is, she has such beautiful, almost dainty, features.*

When we shifted her on the table to move her into the machine, she clutched at the side of the table, as though she was afraid of falling.

I said, "Don't worry, you're safe. We're just moving you."

She had that look—a look every nurse dreads seeing—staring up at the ceiling and into the future, waiting to be taken.

I bent over her and whispered, "Not now. I need to go to lunch."

"Can you pray for me?" she asked.

"What religion are you?"

"Catholic," she answered.

I said, "You and I both believe there's a power greater than we are. You can call upon it right now."

She seemed comforted and let us move her into the machine.

I was anxious to go to lunch, but I wanted to know more about her. *What she was like before this illness? What was she like as a*

She had that look—a look every nurse dreads.

---

wife, a mother, a grandmother? I wanted to see her as a person, not another suffering patient in a hospital gown. *It will only be a few minutes before they come to take her back to her room. Maybe I'll stay and comfort her.* She seemed a little afraid, a little bit alone. But she was just waiting, like me—waiting for the right time, waiting for a sign.

Once she was back on the stretcher and in the hallway, I asked, "What color was your hair?"

"Red," she told me.

"What is your name?"

"Maria Benevenuto," she said.

I was surprised. "Oh!" I said, "I had expected an Irish name to go with your red hair. Have you ever been to Italy?"

"Yes," she said, still staring at something far beyond the ceiling, "It was wonderful. If you ever get the opportunity, you should go to Italy. If you get a chance for anything you can do in your life, and you have the dream, do it."

We chatted for a while about Italy, about her family and about music, which we both loved. After a few minutes, with lunch on my mind, I told her, "I'm going to go; you'll be safe here. Is that ok?" But it wasn't yet time for me to leave Maria.

She blurted out, "Why me? I can't afford to go now. My husband doesn't even know how to pay the bills. He needs me. I want to take my granddaughter to Disneyland for her birthday. I've done everything that was right; I lived my life in a good way. What about those people who never took care of their children, who did the wrong things? They're still here—why me, why now?"

My feet seemed bolted to the floor. My mouth went dry; my heart started to beat very fast. How am I going to answer such a question? How could somebody who barely knew me ask me that question?

I needed to answer her now; I couldn't skirt this question. *I wish I had gotten out the door to lunch before my co-worker called me to assist.* I felt uncomfortable and wished that I was selfish instead of self-full. My answer came from within. I told her, "Based upon my faith, I believe in generational blessings. Everything that you did for your family, for your children and your children's children was because of the blessings in what your parents and their parents before them did.

"As for those people who might not have gotten it right, who might not have done the things they should have for their children,

---

*It takes preparation to trust and embrace
your passion and walk in your true purpose.*

---

it may take them a little bit longer to get to where they need to be—but that's their story; that's their journey. Those people might have had troubles, had obstacles, made mistakes; things might have gone off track for them. It may take them a little bit longer to get where you are right now, but take comfort in knowing that, because of what you did, the blessings will come down on your children and their children and on the lives they will touch."

Maria turned and looked at me and said, "God sent the right nurse."

I answered, "This was just a nurse getting ready to go to lunch who stopped to give a hand."

"No," she insisted, "God sent the right nurse. You were born to do this. You were born to speak into the lives of others."

The faraway look was gone; the color was back in her cheeks. She even smiled.

But I was the grateful one. She had given me the confirmation that I needed. That's the day I believed I could run. Sometimes we have to struggle to find who we are. Sometimes we need to be supported. Sometimes we need others to hold the faith and believe for us. People come into our lives for a season and a reason and it is all just leading up to what's supposed to be. People kept on telling me, "Just be happy you're a nurse; you can make a decent living doing that." But I knew I was called for more and it all started to fall into place.

From that moment on, I started living more intentionally, knowing that I can't just sit on my backside. I started to actively incorporate my life into my teaching. I realized that my own

---

Everything you go through will prepare you for what is to come.

---

personal journey was important. I started to put myself out there instead of letting fear take opportunities away from me. I realized: *The choices I make have a ripple effect and I choose to live and enjoy life.* I began to listen more, to move beyond the stuff—the problems, the noise, the doubts and doubters—around us. My whole head-space is different. And if I get a chance to go to Italy, I'll do it.

It takes preparation to trust and embrace your passion and walk in your true purpose. Everything that happens in our lives, every obstacle, every way that we deal with situations makes us more able to empathize with others.

While you're going through it, it may not seem as if it's easy, or sometimes you may feel a little stuck. Like me, you may think, *I'm here. I'm just waiting for the right time. I'm waiting for the right time to step out and take that leap of faith.* You, too, might need a signal.

While you're waiting, you still have to live your life, knowing the decisions you make will affect your future. If you make mistakes, if you mess up a little bit, that's just a part of life. More than anything else, get the support you need to say, "I'll pick myself up and dust myself off. I need to continue, if I need help I'll ask for help."

In my own life, my employer closed, leaving me jobless and pregnant. I had to start all over again. I went back to school. Twenty years later, the same thing happened when the company I worked for closed. I struggled, but I'd prepared myself. The day came when we had no insurance and had to park the car. *That's life! I'll take the bus.* Maybe you're down, maybe you're up. Maybe you're waiting for the right moment. It's a process; it's life.

Expect to wait, to take some time to trust your passion, to embrace it, to be brave enough to walk into your passion, to walk in your purpose. Rather than being impatient or resentful when things don't happen as fast as you like, trust the process. Believe that everything you go through will prepare you for what is to come.

Live your life fully and intentionally, as it comes to you, and if you ever get the chance, go to Italy.

Sharon Addison is a registered nurse and certified life purpose and career coach who knows firsthand what it's like to pursue your passion and walk in your true purpose. She also graduated from the Connecticut School of Broadcasting with certifications in radio and television production. With more than fifteen years of experience as an independent radio host and producer, she uses her vivacity to captivate the attention of audiences worldwide. Sharon can be heard weekly on radio station 89.1 WFDU FM Thursday mornings 1:15 a.m. to 6:00 a.m. (EST), playing a mixture of Caribbean & World Gospel music, Spotlight on Gospel.

In January 2012, Sharon launched her empowerment company: Your Awesome Power Within Coaching & Consulting™. Her services include private coaching, one- or two-day workshops and four-hour workshops. Connect with Sharon at www.AddisonMediaGroup.com.

Patricia Thompson

My Year of Courage

Looking my husband straight in the eyes, I asked, "I'm still grieving Mom's death two months ago. Now I've found a lump under my arm and need a biopsy. I need to know: Are you going to stand with me or are you leaving?"

"No," answered my husband of thirty-three years, "I won't be with you. I'm leaving."

In my earliest childhood memories, I was always the one who soothed an argument and made peace. When my mother was sick, I took care of her in my little way. I was a very old soul and I seemed to know what to say and do to help others.

In high school, I was secretary of the senior class. I was awarded an academic scholarship to the University of Miami. I met my future husband at church; we married a year after I graduated from high school. We had three beautiful children, but we divorced after seven years. I moved back to Florida to be near my parents. I worked part-time in retail and was assistant to the fashion director at an elegant Miami department store.

I met a struggling young pilot who was going to school at Emery Riddle in Hialeah, Florida, and we began dating. He seemed to care about me and about my children; we remained close as he took one flying job after another, only to be let go because of cutbacks. After we married, we lived in Key West, then Orlando, finally settling down in Memphis, Tennessee, when he found a job with a small-package delivery airline.

Over the next three decades, unknown to me, he built connections with women all over the world. In the years before his retirement, he had established a strong relationship with a Brazilian woman twenty years younger than he. He took all the money he could from our family in Memphis and hid it in Brazil.

When my husband told me he was leaving, I was terrified. I couldn't work; I had not built any savings; I didn't want to be a burden on my children. My husband controlled all the money, and he had moved bank accounts. Without court intervention, I couldn't live; without his insurance, I couldn't get treatment for the cancer. My emotions were in turmoil. I had lost trust in him; my body had betrayed me; my mother had died; and my children did not know how to face the loss not only of their mother, but also of the person they had known as their father for over thirty years.

I call that part of my life the Year of Courage. There was nothing easy about it. The biopsy showed stage-three metastasized breast cancer, but it took six weeks to find the primary tumor. I endured two surgeries, chemotherapy and thirty rounds of radiation.

In the oncologist's office, the poisonous chemicals that would kill good cells along with the bad dripped into my arm. The determinedly cheerful colors of the wallpaper blurred to shades of gray as my eyes brimmed with tears. My skin coloring had

When my husband told me he
was leaving, I was terrified.

changed and I'd lost forty pounds. My hair fell out in handfuls; my eyebrows got thinner and thinner and I could count every eyelash I had left—all three of them. And right now, this very minute, my husband was visiting his mistress. I felt as though I had thrown away thirty-three years of my life and those might be the last years I would have. I asked God, "Why me? I am a good person. I have not hurt others; why me?"

And as clear as a bell, I heard, "Why not you?"

There were signs that ours was not a good marriage, but I had believed in my integrity, and I had transferred my integrity to my husband. When I did that, I gave him more credibility and authentication than he deserved. Because he was a pilot, he could do whatever he chose to do a thousand miles from home and I would never know. I had to believe he was being authentic, or I couldn't have functioned properly. So, I wasn't true to myself. I didn't do the due diligence that I should have. But where would I have found the money to have a detective follow him around the world?

I could not pretend I didn't care about my husband's infidelity, about losing him from my life when I needed him the most. Of course I cared—after over three decades together, you care. But

_____

I began my healing journey by telling myself the truth.

_____

that door had closed—I had to face that truth—and now I had to focus on getting well. I declared, "I want to live, and I want to live in integrity."

I did a lot of praying and working to heal my body, my emotions and my soul, for all had been critically wounded. It took courage to face the treatments my body needed, and perhaps even more courage to look honestly at my emotions and my soul so that they could also heal.

Some of the people who were going through chemotherapy with me did not make it. They would get an infection and, because their immune system was low, they made their transition. Every day, I was frightened this would be my fate. It's very hard to be courageous and hold onto hope when fear is consuming you. And then I got the boost I needed to turn the corner. At the clinic, one of the volunteers came over to me and said, "I'm a seventeen-year survivor." That was so beautiful! She gave me something to believe in.

I began my healing journey by telling myself the truth. When I was married, I was lying to myself that things were better than they were. I should have been preparing myself for a transition out of the marriage.

If you operate in integrity, that means telling the truth, and when you're telling the truth, you only have one story. Once the

---

Holding onto integrity is
always telling the truth.

---

truth is out there, it's out there, and no one needs to go looking for it. You go through the bad part quicker. You come out the other side a little damaged, but not as much as you could be damaged by continuing to lie.

Usually, when you're not operating in integrity, you're operating out of shame or embarrassment or convenience. If you want to operate in integrity, from this moment on, only give the truth as it is, not as you want it to be, not as you perceive what the other person wants.

Too often, we wear a mask. I think it begins in childhood, when we see that somebody else gets praise and credit and we want that, so we start acting like that person. We need to be true to ourselves in how we act. An amazing number of people will honor who you are. And as for those who don't honor who you are, do you need that person in your life if they have a different view of you?

I've survived my Year of Courage with integrity, and I've rebuilt my life. I operate in honesty and truth. When I coach people and talk to people, I believe in diplomacy and I believe in different roads for each person, but I also bring out what their truth is, so they can see it and make decisions based on what's really going on in their lives, so they can build their futures in integrity. We all have difficulties to overcome and problems to solve. The work is easier when you talk with someone who will keep your best interests in mind and help you to find good solutions to bad situations. When you work with a coach, attorney or financial planner to help you find your way through the maze of problems, difficulties will move quickly into solutions.

Holding onto integrity is always telling the truth. If you make a mistake, 'fess up, fix it and move on. The truth is what's so important. If we're honest in our business dealings, if we're honest in our personal relationships, and not trying to be two or three different people—one kind of person at business and a different kind of person at home with the person we love—we can relax and be at peace, because we are authentic.

Above all else, be honest with yourself. You can only live in the world that actually is—not in a dream of perfection that does not exist. You can only love yourself or your soul mate as he or she actually is—not as you expect or hope or imagine. And when the crisis comes, for crises come to all of us, your habit of integrity will give you the courage to emerge from it—whole and wholly you.

Patricia Thompson is transformational speaker and a Certified Dream Coach™. Trained by Marcia Weider, she has received Silva Mind Training and Psych-K training. Memphis Woman magazine twice honored Patricia as one of "50 Women Who Make a Difference." She co-founded the largest art organization in the Memphis/Germantown area and founded and was president of the Coalition for Visual Arts and of The Network for Health Insurance Continuance, with which she was an advocate for heathcare coverage to the Tennessee legislature for five years. Connect with Patricia at www.DiscoverYourFuture.net.

Mari Santo-Domingo

It Doesn't Matter Where You Start

Have you ever thought that everything around you is not working to your advantage? Have you ever questioned why you are where you are today? Have you ever wondered if you have been the author of your own downfall?

My entire life fit into two suitcases and while I waited for a taxi at the airport in Puerto Rico, I thought, *Okay, Mari. Here you are, back home, with nothing. What are you going to do now? Where are you going to start?* Sighing heavily as I looked up at the azure blue sky, the sun beating down on me, I checked my watch and took stock of just how I had come to be here.

I grew up in a small town on the island of Puerto Rico, and it is very interesting how you think and behave when you are an islander. You think you are the center of the world and sometimes you might behave like it. It is not until you leave the island that you will realize the world is as big as your reality. I had left the island in 1985 looking for a change, better opportunities, a better lifestyle—the American dream!

My reality when I moved to Miami was: by myself, on my own. My attitude: Let's make things happen, let's start knocking on doors. I was a competitive workaholic; I had no boundaries and loved challenges. I had many doors closed in my face, but I always repeated to myself the advice my grandfather had shared with me:

"Mari, if you know how to knock on doors, if you know how to be visible, what seems impossible will show up; it doesn't matter where you start or where you come from."

By the time I had been living in Miami for six years, I'd certainly taken to city life. I'd started an image consulting business with a friend and we were doing great, on our way to becoming a huge success—until one day, she told me she would have to bow out. As it stood, I couldn't afford the office costs on my own and shortly after my partner left I was forced to close the business for good.

With the business gone, I had no source of income; I started searching for a job. Meanwhile, I had to resort to living off my credit cards. In those days, I didn't know any better—to me, a wallet full

---

I was a competitive workaholic; I had
no boundaries and loved challenges.

---

of credit cards and store cards for every single establishment was like a status tag. It meant that I was good, that I was doing well and that I was *better.* There are consequences to every decision: I knew that then, but what other option did I have?

Within three months, I had lost everything. Not only my business and my perfect credit score, but also my confidence and self-worth. Luckily, I had a friend with an apartment she wasn't using who kindly offered to let me use it in my hour of need. I walked into her six-hundred-square-foot efficiency studio in two minds: On one hand, I was grateful not to be completely destitute, to have a roof over my head and a bed to sleep in. On the other, I was in financial ruin and had no idea how to go about piecing the tatters of my life back together.

I was blessed to have people around me who cared and one friend in particular, Ingrid, made a point of calling me almost every day to check in and see how I was doing. She took me by the hand and allowed me to be in a space where I wasn't thinking to myself, *Mari, you're alone.* It was another friend—Lissette—who introduced me to her industry, an industry that gave me the tools and proven systems to build a home-based business. It was also this friend who finally told me that I had to face the facts of my situation as it stood right at that moment.

When she found out that I only had enough money for pizza, corn flakes and Coca-Cola, she looked me right in the eye and said, "Mari, you have to go back home."

I had always been so sure, so completely certain that I would not go back to my parents in Puerto Rico, but at that point there really was no other option left for me. Of course, it wasn't as though I could just pluck the money for a plane ticket out of thin air and, knowing that my parents were going through some big financial hardships of their own at the time, I was resolutely against asking them for the money. Thankfully, a friend from college was able to lend me the money.

During my first couple of weeks back, I took the time to consider what it was that I truly wanted out of life. In all of the jobs I'd had since leaving home, I'd started out at the bottom and worked my way to the top. When in big need, the world doesn't need to know—applying for a "cameo" role in the movie of your life is not

---

Within three months, I had lost everything.

---

going to kill you, but staying "cameo" will. In my first job, I applied to be a receptionist and six months later I was sales manager. I learned that working at the front desk you will know everybody and have the opportunity to study all departments and make the right connections to move ahead.

Even with this level of success, there had always seemed to be something missing, something that would never quite "click." It was being around my parents again, who were entrepreneurs and had had their own business for twenty-five years at this point, that helped slot into place the last piece of the puzzle. When I realized it, I laughed out loud—it should have been so obvious! I'd always wanted to be well-known, admired, and remembered—I wasn't ever someone who was happy to settle for mediocrity—but I'd never been able to decide on a career path. I realized it was because I was meant to be an entrepreneur, not an employee.

Having that realization was like the loudest wake-up call. I needed a major attitude adjustment: I was back to square one, completely starting over from zero point, and I had to become an observer of the uncomfortable situation I was facing in order to see everything clearly. I had to step back and say, "I don't want to be at the mercy of anyone or anything ever again."

There's nothing like a bad experience to put you off a particular course of action, but the option you refuse to consider based on a past experience may often be the most profitable one to take. Saying, "I won't do that again," or, "I won't go back home," just because things didn't work as you expected simply skews your

---

"What if the next door is the one?"

---

vision and renders you less able to recognize an opportunity when it occurs. I'd had it all and lost it all—now, I had to completely overhaul myself: I had to develop my character; drop pettiness and my reliance on the image I had of myself; train my mind; and listen to and enjoy my life.

The industry Lissette had exposed me to while I'd still been in Miami suddenly looked like the beacon lighting my way. It allowed me to be exposed to coaches, trainers, and mentors—people who had done it before and could show me the path. But first, I realized, I had to start knocking on those doors again. I had to learn everything I could from the people I earned access to by being visible and take it all on board so that I didn't have to reinvent the wheel.

It took discipline to conquer the nagging voices in my mind: I was too critical, always thinking that everything had to be perfect, but I learned to embrace my imperfections. Les Brown once said, "Just because you don't see it, it doesn't mean it's not coming" and I finally understood that some problems are not going to be solved— they will only be outlived. But in order to outlive the problems, I at least had to be present and visible for them and learn from each experience.

Action must follow learning and, after my setback and experiences in Miami, I took everything I had learned from my mentors and coaches and put it to work. I settled back home, married my soul mate, Miguel—who has also been my business partner for twenty years—and together we built a multi-million-dollar consulting business; broke company sales records; and helped several companies launch their line of products, programs and systems into the Hispanic market not only in the island but on the mainland, too.

Everything will start not only with you, but with your capacity to show up and be visible in your leadership. A home-based business may not be for everybody, but *anybody* can learn the skills and disciplines to grow a business that is sustainable and profitable. You have to stand out, be different, noteworthy and unforgettable—these are qualities you need in order not only to knock on all the doors you can, but to keep those doors from being closed on you.

When I was focused on what I needed, what I didn't have, what I was missing, everything stopped. But the minute I started thinking and strategizing on how to bless others, help and serve them, build and empower them, the phone started ringing. Referrals, prospects, new programs, new opportunities, new proposals and deals were on doorstep.

You will never know what is on the other side of the door, but instead of being scared of it, embrace the unknown. Take risks and don't be afraid of failure—your eagerness to take on uncertainty, backed by thorough preparation, will motivate you and those around you to help you rise above and become visible in life and leadership. The question shouldn't be, "When do I stop knocking on doors?" The question should be, "What if the next door is the one?"

George Eliot once wrote, "It is never too late to be what you might have been." Today I let inspiration come from the connection to the most powerful light that emanates from my heart's radiance where the Creator seeded our divine purpose. Now, living in my purpose and doing what I was meant to do, I realize more strongly than ever that it doesn't matter *when* or *where* you start—just that you start at all.

Mari is an energetic, passionate bilingual leader and "speakpreneur" who has inspired thousands of women to take action. Her keynotes, trainings, programs and systems are based on over twenty years as a successful entrepreneur. She has been recognized as a gifted teacher and expert in the field of VISIBLE Leadership. Through her experience and influence as a corporate trainer she opened and developed the Hispanic market for one of America's greatest brands: BeautiControl. As a style and image expert she contributed to many local and national magazines and was a TV host and producer. She is a founding member of Lisa Nichol's Global Leadership Program and of M. Koenigs and P. Hendrickson Business Accelerator Mastermind and is a graduate of CEO Space. She has served on the Board of the Women Helping Others Foundation.

Mari is writing her first book about her life's calling: to work, coach and guide women who have been, are or aspire to be in a leadership position; women whose busy lifestyles might make them feel unappreciated, unaccomplished, overwhelmed, but who still want to SHOW UP, women who want to become powerful, impactful, inspiring and VISIBLE leaders. Make your own start at www. WomenInLeadershipAcademy.com.

Carol Rydell

Know Thyself, Love Thyself, Value Thyself

"I can't, I can't, I just CAN'T anymore," I sobbed. I lay curled on the bathroom floor where I had collapsed hours ago, the cool tile chilling the puddle of tears under my face. *There's nothing. No future. Just pain.* I felt betrayed on every level. Worst of all, I had betrayed myself.

My second husband, Mike, and I had met when I was twenty-two and very successful as a young single woman. We were passionately in love with each other and we had built two businesses together. But, when we started having money troubles, he had insisted that I should become an escort to help pay the bills.

He kept talking about my body being of value, my body being of value, my body being of value— it was the first time anybody ever talked about my having anything of value.

I was already working eighteen hours a day in our businesses and I was exhausted. But we really needed money, and this seemed like the most efficient way to get caught up. At the same time, I felt a sense of shame: *I was raised in a good home. I shouldn't be doing this. Isn't this illegal?* And I felt something totally new: a sense of power in the knowledge that I had something of value. That was intoxicating. It didn't have anything to do with the men; it was all my own. And it kept me going through six months of humiliation until Mike came to me and told me he was having an affair. Something broke inside me then. I realized that all I had done for love had been for someone who didn't love me or value me at all. *I have been living in the trash.*

"I love Mike so much and I am so unhappy because I have to divorce him," I had told my father tearfully, soon after Mike's admission.

He screamed back at me, "What's wrong with you? Get over it and move on!" He was just unable to acknowledge or validate my emotion.

My dad was a Holocaust survivor and my mom's parents were immigrants. Life for them was about survival and working hard, very hard. Any emotion or need I had beyond the basics was off the table. If I expressed upset about something, my parents would say, "How dare you?" Hard work and education were important.

Thus, I always felt that there was something wrong with me, because I felt so deeply and I wanted love so badly. I couldn't turn off my feelings. I craved relationship, yet all my relationships felt bankrupt. *Why don't I matter?* I asked over and over again, through my childhood, through my teens, through my broken

---

**He had insisted that I should become
an escort to help pay the bills.**

---

marriage. What Mike and I had wasn't really love, but at the time it felt more like love than anything I'd ever known. That's why I thought selling my body to support my husband was somehow okay. I'd just been glad I could do something to help.

After talking with my dad, I cried all the way home, mourning what I thought had been a marriage. More devastating, though, was the grief I felt for myself. *Who am I? How did I get here? What the hell happened to my life? I don't know who I am. I have to divorce Mike. I have to divorce this whole way of life or I'll never survive!* I had never felt such pain. I was broken on the inside and out, and I didn't know how I would go on. But I did know: *I have to take care of myself.* "I have to divorce Mike, for me!" I declared. Even as I said it, the tightness in my solar plexus eased. I felt my heart beginning to expand.

Lying there on the cold white tile, for the first time in my life, I made the choice to value myself.

In that moment, I finally saw that I could only have a healthy relationship with another after coming into relationship with myself. I realized, the day I hit bottom, that I needed to begin that process, no matter how scary it would be. Everywhere I went, I had carried a sense of unworthiness; it had affected the choices I

I take myself out of the game when I don't value myself.

---

made, the paths I took, my deepest feelings about what love was. While Mike and I were together, I believed that if I worked hard enough, if I did everything I was asked, someday I would finally be a lovable person and that Mike would love me even more. But now I saw that nothing would change until I loved myself.

To begin, I needed to be able to accept all those parts of myself that I had spent years pushing away. I needed to be able to see the wounds, the pain and the shame of all my life choices—especially the ones I had made to just survive—as beautiful also. In bringing together all the parts of myself with love and acceptance, I began to create the magic and the magnificence of my life. Each experience has been a facet of the precious diamond that I am.

Deciding to leave Mike and strike out on my own was a first step. But the first big leg-up in developing my self-worth came from going back to school. I had never taken tests well, but I took real estate exams and—Oh my gosh—I passed! *I studied and I passed? I think I'll take the next state's test.* I passed. *If I can do this, I must be better than I thought I was. I can go back to school!* I had expected to fail, but I went on to get my accounting degree and pass the CPA exam.

I continued to create opportunities for accomplishment that stretched me. Along the way, I carefully orchestrated situations in which I could practice exercising trust in my own instincts and following my heart. It was a huge effort to learn to live for me and nobody else, to learn to love and value myself not just for my body or my ability to work hard, but for myself as a person, from the inside out. And so now, I attract experiences where I get to show up for myself and know myself better, rather than hand over all my power to other people. And I keep learning that I take myself out of the game when I don't value myself.

In my earlier life, I hadn't known that I felt powerless; but the way I acted showed that I did. Now, I get to use that first experience of discovering personal power as a guiding feeling even though, ironically, it came during those months when I worked as an escort. I know now that if I want to go to a core place of strength and solidity in myself, I can call up that feeling of power in my body in a new, self-loving way and it will carry me forward into the future. That technique is a big part of what I teach as a mentor now. It's tapping into those feelings, not the stories around them, which can provide a guidepost to help us know whether we're on or off our own path. When we tap into that feeling again, we know, *YES. This is it.*

If you are looking outside yourself for a sense of self-worth, it is time to stop. You can't wait for the prince to come and save you. It's really about creating, even with many little steps, your own unique pathway to what YOU consider success. If you don't value yourself, no one will! If you know, value, trust and love yourself, your outer world will reflect your inner landscape.

Your experiences, gifts, talents, beauty, body and message are precious and important.

Try really looking at your own stories, and the tapes that play in your head, while saying, "Hmm, what's the thread here? What am I learning from all these experiences in which I am the common denominator?" Once you know yourself, you can rewrite your story from what's really true for YOU. "What am I learning? What kind of school am I in?" For me, the school is power and value. Every experience teaches me those things.

Only we take ourselves out of the game; nobody else needs to do it for us. So make a decision, a commitment to you—no matter what! Decide who you want to be and how you want to feel from the inside out. The commitment becomes the fuel that moves you forward. Get to know yourself: your purpose, your values, your spiritual source. Accept who you are completely, then give yourself permission to dream and change the story. Develop relationship with and trust your inner authority; your inner guidance system will help you remove obstacles and create relationships that truly support you. Reevaluate often to determine that you are on your own path. Communicate clearly and ask for what you want. And celebrate yourself for making the brave choice to live.

In my old story, I hit every wall that I could recognize. Following everybody else's pathway, I found myself at the bottom of the barrel, depleted and thinking, *Wow! This is not me! What's true for me? What's true for ME?* That was many years and a third marriage ago, and I've now been with my beloved Gary for over

---

Your experiences, gifts, talents, beauty, body and message are precious and important.

---

sixteen years. Ours was the first relationship I didn't just jump right into, because I was consciously protecting myself—not from a wounded place, but from a place of self-love. The first time I ever shared my story, I really felt the sacred trust in which Gary held my truth, without judgment. He said, "Thank you so much. I am so honored you shared that with me—it makes me love you even more."

Valuing yourself is like being a diplomat. Diplomats can be open-hearted and open-minded while listening to others, yet they don't give themselves away. They remain receptive and in their power, and then they present their own points. They come to some form of agreement—or not! They value what they bring to the table or the relationship just as much as they value what others might bring.

Now, I experience sheer abundance and joy. I am able to help others step into their own magnificence, because I have lived these transformations myself. I can serve joyfully, because I have learned my own value and truth.

As you step more fully into your own beauty, becoming anchored in who you are, know that no one can ever, ever take that wisdom—or your power—away from you. I stand ready to assist, to celebrate and to witness the flowering of your power.

Carol Rydell is a soul-inspired "Wealth Mentor" and a pioneer in raising both the individual and collective consciousness of how we "do" money, business and spirituality. For over thirty years in business, she's been on a mission to guide women back to claiming their inner and outer wealth. She is the creator of "7 Keys to Own Your Magnificence, Master Your Money & Live Your Wealth™" which has helped countless successful women, luminaries and organizations to significantly increase their return of investment (ROI) as well as their "Diamond Wealth." Connect with Carol at www.YouAreDiamond.com.

Linda S. Crawford

Finding My Essence of Self Through Purpose

As a Southern woman moving from Florida in the 1980s, I was very excited by relocating to Southern California: sunshine, beautiful coastlines and many professional opportunities. I figured I would be running into movie stars in fancy restaurants and living the good life just as I had seen in the movies.

I started my professional career working for a leading recreational vehicle corporation in Riverside. This was my first exposure to people who earned a lot of money, and I got to work alongside executives and see how they lived. I worked there for five years in data processing as a trainer and IT troubleshooter before separating from my husband, who then moved back to Florida. I was truly alone for the first time in my life.

Luckily, I landed a job as an engineer—the only female engineer on a team of forty—with the second largest computer manufacturer in the United States. I needed technical training, but I also knew I could make more money and live securely by working in field service. It took two years before I decided to pursue a sales career, marketing various service offerings for the corporation, and another year until I felt ready for the big league: selling hardware technology.

I worked in various sales positions for another ten years, continuing to be promoted, winning awards and year-end trips.

But as the quotas kept rising, so did the pressure to perform and compete against my peers. As a sales professional, you feel you are on a continuous hamster wheel to keep your deals lined up in case some are delayed or won by the competition. You have a lot of highs and lows both emotionally and mentally, not to mention what it does to the cortisol levels in your body due to the stress.

Knowing that I needed to stay healthy in order to compete against my colleagues, in 1995 I decided to finish my degrees in business and nutrition. I started a part-time nutritional counseling business and focused on working with employees and friends who were asking how they could increase their energy like me and "feel younger." But I soon realized that they were only looking for that silver bullet to lose weight and increase their energy—they did not have the time to deal with any lifestyle changes that would allow them to become healthier the old-fashioned way, through diet and exercise. It was disheartening to watch.

My ambition was telling me to push on and I allowed my health to take a back seat in order to further my career. I also ended a long-term relationship with a man who had become my best friend and confidante—a very emotional decision for me, since he had acted as the calm in my storm for many years. I continued to be

When the symptoms began, I was completely unprepared.

successful monetarily, but worked under tremendous pressure, becoming a road warrior to keep up with the demands of my position. But I knew in my heart there was something greater, a deeper gift within me to offer the world in my lifetime.

When the symptoms began, I was completely unprepared. It was 2004, and I had started working for a billion-dollar telecom manufacturer. I had reached the height of my career monetarily but made no time for vacations or relaxation and stress was taking its toll. I had been noticing patches of dry skin developing on my face; I was feeling more and more fatigued on the road. I decided to make an appointment with an acupuncturist to relieve some of my stress. Though the treatment helped, it proved only to be a temporary fix for a much bigger underlying problem. At the time, I did not realize that this was the beginning of my body trying to tell me that I was triggering responses from my immune system due to the stress levels I was feeling daily. Little did I know that I was developing a gluten intolerance and food allergies that would continue for years.

I had built my entire reputation around my career and, by 2010, I was working for a billion-dollar health publishing corporation, selling online training and services to health systems. Since my allergy symptoms had begun in 2004, they had worsened dramatically—but so had my denial of their root cause. My career had become my life and, in my mind, financial ruin was the worst possible thing that could ever happen to someone. So I blindly carried on and paid no mind to how my body was reacting to my poor diet, lack of sleep and the ever-increasing demands I placed upon my immune system. I was so focused on competing and on monetary gain that I stopped worrying about my health.

During the 2010 holiday season, my sales manager was afraid he would not achieve his year-end sales goal and announced that all vacations were canceled. My holiday season flew by like the blink of an eye as I raced to close eleven deals in order to make my quota. The stress and anxiety were affecting me worse than ever. I was unable to enjoy the few holiday parties I attended with the man in my life, because afterward I would experience rash breakouts, stomach cramps and fatigue. *What am I eating or doing that is causing these serious reactions?* I wondered.

While working late one night, I began to take a hard look at my life and how my body was reacting to the choices I had made. My health had deteriorated so badly that the only thing I could attribute it to was the continuing stress my high-pressured career was causing me. I began resent my job and my employer.

On the other hand, wasn't money the only measure of success that really mattered? It certainly was in the male-dominated business world I grew up in. I remembered my mother struggling with money, having had four children. I watched her suffer monetarily many times, because she would take care of her kids' needs above her own.

"Linda, make sure you establish your own credit and make your own money," she always told me. "Do not ever have to depend on anyone to take care of you."

Who am I if not a financial success at this point in my career? I asked myself, and what a powerful question that was!

I was so focused on competing and on monetary gain that I stopped worrying about my health.

I spent days this way, sifting through layers of emotional, spiritual and financial anguish in realizing I might have to start my career over again. I felt helpless. *How will I ever succeed again?* I thought. *Who will want to listen to or work with me? I feel like a failure to myself, but how much more can I take? Even though it is the only career I have known, is it time to move on?*

I had to find a way to stop suffering and start living my life again. My career was no longer fulfilling; my health was continuing to fail. It had knocked me to my knees with a force that threw me down into darkness, pain and fear the like of which I had never experienced. Some days I could not recognize myself through the depression. Sometimes I felt angry for allowing this to happen to me. I had been a healthy, vibrant woman my entire life. Many days I questioned God, and prayed for divine guidance to remove the fear in my heart.

Those were the worst days of my life. Yet, somehow, they were also the best days of my life. There came a night when I was lying in bed going through another round of soul-searching, asking myself, *If I choose to walk away from corporate life because of my health, what am I going to do for the rest of my career?* I needed to find something that would not only allow me to serve others in my community, but also to heal myself. What more did I have to offer to this world that would make a deeper impact on people's lives?

I got out of bed, sat down, and wrote down all the strengths I had developed through my life experiences and education. Being able to connect with people and help transform their lives in a positive way, inspiring them to reclaim their right to good health and to shine their brightest light in the world was a talent I had been given. But I had stepped away from this truth and had not trusted it enough to focus on it full-time.

Being a high-achieving performer in the corporate world had been a cover for my deep-seated fear: *When is money and success ever going to be enough for me to feel secure within myself?* I was all I had to count on. Money and success had been my security. I had no family or any other financial support coming my way. I sat back and looked at my list of strengths. I realized that though I felt helpless, I did not feel powerless.

Finally, I made the decision to leave corporate life. Now I had no reliable source of income and I had to rely completely on divine guidance to help me navigate the new and unknown terrain of my career. What new business was trying to emerge through me? I found an inner strength, confidence and wisdom I had never felt until now. So I promised God that I would use my talents and skills in the highest service to others if I could realize my true calling. I

*Throw caution to the wind and
find your true purpose!*

prayed on that request and went to bed. By the next morning, after my meditation, I had my answer.

I decided to go back to school to learn how to professionally coach people on understanding their food allergens, detox concerns and how lifestyle directly affects health, emotions and overall wellness. It was truly a leap of faith for me; but if I didn't believe in myself, who else would? I slowly came to realize that my purpose was to educate and inspire others to eat healthy food, eliminate toxins and live active lifestyles in order to live their best lives.

It was a major mind shift, because my selling style had always been to focus on the products or services of my employer. Now, by the grace of God, I got to channel all of my energy into the gift I had been given for helping others to heal, transform and live healthy lives. My strengths had always been there, but I had never developed the eyes to see them. My gluten intolerance and food allergies had been a wake-up call, a blessing in disguise to show me that though my career rewarded me monetarily, it took a little of my joy and peace of mind every day.

I got caught up in striving for greater and greater financial success, because it gave a false sense of security that I bought into, and in the process, I lost my sense of self. Once I became honest with myself, I saw the truth that selling to health systems to help them save money was not a true calling for me and did not inspire me to greatness. I realized that I had not been living with purpose.

Living today with purpose allows me to live in the true essence of who I am meant to be in this lifetime. So throw caution to the wind and find your true purpose! Don't be afraid of failure. Instead, learn from it and keep moving forward. Facing failure is sometimes the new beginning of the path to what you are meant to do with your life.

If you sat down to write out a list of your strengths, what new vision would you see for your life? How could you not only serve others, but also find your sense of self along the way? Would you find the path you have always been meant to walk? I hope so.

LINDA S. CRAWFORD

Linda Crawford is a gluten/food allergen/chemical toxin specialist who offers coaching and consulting regarding gluten-free eating, food allergens and chemical toxin reduction in the body and the home. She received her bachelor's degrees in business and nutrition and in 1995 started her first business as a nutritional counselor. For more information on her coaching and consulting services, visit www. LifestyleChanges2Health.com. She is also a healthy gourmet cook who works with clients to help them understand ingredient labeling, pantry clearing and kitchen setup. She conducts home cooking classes and menu planning to uncover disguised chemical toxins, reactionary foods, sugars and carbs in everyday products. For more information on her classes and parties, visit www.PleasinThePalate.com.

Sandra Yancey

Conclusion

This past year I went on a thirty-three-city, six-month tour of the United States and Canada for eWomenNetwork's Annual Women's Success Summit. During this time, my mother fell critically and terminally ill and four months later, our precious family dog, Cinco, passed away from the same illness. In both cases, they deteriorated rapidly over a period of days.

It was a difficult time, and there were moments when it seemed like my grief would consume me. Yet once I was able to step out of it and breathe again, the message was clear: Make sure you're doing everything that is important to you, because you really don't know how much time you have. In a matter of hours or days, a seemingly frivolous symptom can turn into something catastrophic.

This was the beginning of my transformation. As I traveled North America, listening to the diverse stories of women who were honoring a calling, women who were striving for something better or searching for the courage to dream bigger and women who were knocking it out of the park running highly successful businesses, I realized I was not alone. So many of us are experiencing sweeping changes in our lives and in our businesses. It's only natural that we would want to take stock, come back to center and ask the big questions:

Am I fulfilled?

Am I doing the work I was put on this planet to do?

Am I embracing all of who I really am?

I began to look at every area of my life to determine if I was on the right path, or just simply marching down a path that no longer served me or enabled me to best serve the planet.

Watching my mother deteriorate broke my heart. It also *opened* my heart and allowed me to get in touch with the desires, dreams, ideas and feelings I had buried while caught up in the hurriedness of life.

I realized that while I had done a lot of keynotes, led masterminds and facilitated learning on some level, I hadn't created any new training programs in well over a decade.

The last thirteen years have given me the opportunity to learn some powerful lessons—business lessons and personal lessons—and once I opened my heart, it was clear that I *missed* creating training programs that brought real, powerful transformation to the lives of other people.

They say from whom much is given, much is required. I've been given a lot—not just money and extraordinary business success, but also the opportunity to learn and really understand

---

Start seeing obstacles, barriers and setbacks as a chance to learn more about yourself and your business.

---

the meanings of life, lessons I believe I am now required to bring to entrepreneurs across the world. I've begun to develop trainings that would not only deliver the fundamental skills and tools necessary to grow a business, but also the deeper level, inner work that provides entrepreneurs with a heartfelt understanding of how they may be holding themselves back from greatness.

As I said in the Introduction about the fantastic stories in this book, whatever you come up against in the pursuit of your goals—be it personal tragedy, or rejection, or lack of time, money or other resources—use it as an opportunity for personal transformation. Open *your* heart to dreams long buried. You deserve to feel fulfilled in all areas of life.

Start seeing obstacles, barriers and setbacks as a chance to learn more about yourself and your business, and then use all you've learned to your advantage. When you shift your perception about all that you think stands in your way, you begin to realize that, in fact, you are not succeeding against all odds, but turning the negative odds in your favor!

It's your time to soar, so spread your wings and take flight!

In gratitude,
Sandra Yancey

About Sandra Yancey

S andra Yancey is an award-winning entrepreneur, international speaker, philanthropist, movie producer, bestselling author and transformational expert who is dedicated to helping women achieve and succeed. She is the CEO and founder of eWomenNetwork, a complete success system for connecting and promoting women and their businesses worldwide.

Sandra is the bestselling author of *Succeeding In Spite of Everything* and *Relationship Networking: The Art of Turning Contacts Into Connections;* and she is co-author, with Julie Ziglar Norman, of *Mastering Moxie: From Contemplating to Creating Absolute Success.* Sandra is also featured in *Chicken Soup for the Entrepreneur's Soul,* which showcases some of the top entrepreneurs in North America.

Sandra Yancey

Founder and CEO, eWomenNetwork

Internationally-Acclaimed and Award Winning Entrepreneur

CNN American Hero

Bestselling author

Featured in *Chicken Soup for the Entrepreneur's Soul*

Philanthropist & Movie Producer

To apply and receive your complimentary consultation and gift of my exclusive C.A.S.H Formula, go to **www.GlowCoach.com**

my exclusive

G.L.O.W.
COACHING PROGRAM

Working with thousands of entrepreneurs from all over North America, I understand how easy it is to get off track.

I am thrilled to offer you the opportunity to access my personal success and accountability coaching program. It's called G.L.O.W. and it means Generating Lasting Opportunities & Wealth.

If you know you are ready to soar and succeed at your optimum level, then I invite you to take the most powerful first step in your personal breakthrough and apply for my exclusive G.L.O.W. Coaching program.

You will find that my G.L.O.W. Coaching program is personally inspired and tailor-made for your success. I have arranged a complimentary consultation with a select member of my team and, as a bonus when you apply, you'll receive my popular C.A.S.H Formula program which teaches you powerful strategies to generate more revenue in your business.